Lean In Construction
(Key to Improvements in Time, Cost and Quality)

By Ade Asefeso MCIPS MBA

Copyright 2014 by Ade Asefeso MCIPS MBA
All rights reserved.

ISBN-13: 978-1499357387
ISBN-10: 1499357389

Publisher: AA Global Sourcing Ltd
Website: http://www.aaglobalsourcing.com

Table of Contents

Disclaimer 5
Dedication 6
Chapter 1: Introduction 7
Chapter 2: A Paradigm Shifting Concept 13
Chapter 3: Integrated Project Delivery 19
Chapter 4: Last Planner System 23
Chapter 5: Lean Construction Eliminates Waiting 27
Chapter 6: Performance Focused Lean Construction Application 31
Chapter 7: Collaboration and Lean Construction 35
Chapter 8: Three Lean Tools for Improving Construction Reliability 37
Chapter 9: 5S System on the Construction Job Site 43
Chapter 10: Steps to Sustaining the 5S System on the Jobsite 47
Chapter 11: Value Stream Maps 51
Chapter 12: A3 Strategy Deployment 55
Chapter 13: Construction-Sales Gemba Walks 57
Chapter 14: The 7 Wastes on the Construction Site 61
Chapter 15: Examples of Motion Waste on the Jobsite 63
Chapter 16: The Cost of Second Time Quality 67
Chapter 17: Construction Cost Reduction Starts on the Jobsite 71
Chapter 18: Kaizen and Plan-Do-Check-Adjust 75
Chapter 19: Creating the Fishbone and 5-Why Analysis 81

Chapter 20: Applying Lean Thinking in Construction 85
Chapter 21: Lean Construction Supply Chain 93
Chapter 22: Lean Construction Waste Management 99
Chapter 23: Manufacturing Process Versus the Construction 109
Chapter 24: Barriers to Implementing Lean Construction in the United Kingdom 111
Chapter 25: Lean Construction if Not Now, When? 123
Chapter 26: Lean Construction Frequently Ask Questions 129

Disclaimer

This publication is designed to provide competent and reliable information regarding the subject matter covered. However, it is sold with the understanding that the author and publisher are not engaged in rendering professional advice. The authors and publishers specifically disclaim any liability that is incurred from the use or application of contents of this book.

If you purchased this book without a cover you should be aware that this book may have been stolen property and reported as "unsold and destroyed" to the publisher. In this case neither the author nor the publisher has received any payment for this "stripped book."

Dedication

This book is dedicated to my family and friends who seems to have been sent here to teach me something about who I am supposed to be. They have nurtured me, challenged me, and even opposed me.... But at every juncture has taught me!

This book is dedicated to my lovely boys, Thomas, Michael and Karl. Teaching them to manage their finance will give them the lives they deserve. They have taught me more about life, presence, and energy management than anything I have done in my life.

Chapter 1: Introduction

Applying Lean thinking has transformed many industries and its implementation in construction industry has now started to show the potential benefits. The Lean approach is the only way that improvements in time, cost and quality can be made simultaneously without trade off. Lean construction focuses on delivering precisely what the client and end-user want. Its application requires a fresh approach in thinking about the complete process from design through to construction in order to remove waste, to create "continuous flow" and to radically enhance value to the customer.

We identified Lean as one of the key approaches that could lead to great improvements in quality and efficiency. The main principles of Lean are:
1. Specify value from the end customer's perspective.
2. Clearly identify the process that delivers customer values and eliminate all non value adding steps.
3. Make the remaining value adding steps flow without interruption.
4. Let the customer pull; don't make anything until it is needed, then make it quickly.
5. Pursue perfection by continuous improvement.

These principles are now being applied to construction in terms that are easily understood. Impressive benefits being demonstrated by the early practitioners have led to an increasing demand for information on what is involved and how to proceed.

Lean Construction is a way to do more and more with less and less; less effort, less equipment, less time and less space whilst providing customers with exactly what they want.

A Lean system, process, and organisation is one that is waste free. Lean is not about size or number of people employed. A reduction in employees may cut costs, and eliminate the waste of those employees, but does not decrease the proportion of waste to value adding within the organisation or process. Most waste is through products waiting to be worked on by succeeding activities.

Types of waste

Waste can take on many forms within the building process. Below are some common examples:
1. Building ahead of demand/time.
2. Waiting (people, material, information, for the next operation).
3. Unnecessary transport (double handling).
4. Inappropriate processing (larger machines, unnecessary steps, machines not quality capable, over design).
5. Material stocks (early deliveries, storage space, deterioration).
6. Unnecessary motions (ergonomics, bending, reaching).
7. Building defective parts/sections.
8. Waste of untapped human potential.

The impact of Lean

Lean thinking changes the process of product delivery and therefore should give revolutionary improvements. It has been described as delivering "more-for-less". Value Engineering (VE), on the other hand, provides savings through changes to the actual product and not necessarily the process. VE has therefore been described as delivering "less-for-less".

A new paradigm

The mismatch between the conceptual models and observed reality underscored the lack of robustness in the existing constructs and signaled the need for a theory of production in construction therefore we will use the ideal production system embodied in the Toyota Production System to develop a more overarching production management paradigm for project-based production systems where production is conceptualized in three complementary ways, namely, as a Transformation (T), as a Flow (F), and as Value generation (V).

Transformation is the production of inputs into outputs.

Flow can be defined as "Movement that is smooth and uninterrupted, as in the flow of work from one crew to the next or the flow of value at the Pull of the customer."

Value is "What the Customer is actually paying for the project to produce and install.

Lean construction can be describe as way to design production systems to minimize waste of materials, time, and effort in order to generate the maximum possible amount of value. Designing a production system to achieve the stated ends is only possible through the collaboration of all project participants (Owner, Constructors, Facility Managers, End-user) at early stages of the project. This goes beyond the contractual arrangement of design/build or constructability reviews where constructors, and sometime facility managers, merely react to designs instead of informing and influencing the design.

Lean construction recognizes that desired ends affect the means to achieve these ends, and that available means will affect realized ends. Essentially, Lean construction aims to embody the benefits of the Master Builder concept.

Lean construction draws upon the principles of project-level management and upon the principles that govern production-level management. Lean construction recognizes that any successful project undertaking will inevitably involve the interaction between project and production management.

Lean construction supplements traditional construction management approaches with:
1. Two critical and necessary dimensions for successful capital project delivery by requiring the deliberate consideration of material and information flow and value generation in a production system.
2. Different project and production management (planning-execution-control) paradigms.

While Lean construction is identical to Lean production in spirit, it is different in how it was conceived as well how it is practiced. There is a view that "adaptation" of Lean Manufacturing/Production forms the basis of Lean Construction. My view is very different, with the origin of Lean construction arising mainly from the need for a production theory in construction and anomalies that were observed in the reliability of weekly production planning.

Getting work to flow reliably and predictably on a construction site requires the impeccable alignment of the entire supply chain responsible for constructed facilities such that value is maximized and waste is minimized. With such a broad scope, it is fair to say that tools found in Lean Manufacturing and Lean Production, as practiced by Toyota and others, have been adapted to be used in the fulfillment of Lean construction principles. Total Quality management (TQM), Statistical process control (SPC), six-sigma, have all found their way into Lean construction. Similarly, tools and methods found in other areas, such as in social science and business, are used where they are applicable. The tools and methods in construction management, such as work breakdown structure, etc., are also utilized in Lean construction implementations. The three unique tools and methods that were specifically conceived for Lean construction are the Last Planner System, Target Value Design, and the Lean Project Delivery System.

Chapter 2: A Paradigm Shifting Concept

Lean construction is a philosophy based on the concepts of Lean manufacturing. It is about managing and improving the construction process to profitably deliver what the customer needs.

Construction and manufacturing differ significantly in the physical features of the end product. In manufacturing, finished goods generally can be moved as a whole to retailers or end customers. Construction, on the other hand, deals with larger units that cannot be transported. Lean construction is a translation and adaptation of Lean manufacturing principles and practices to the end-to-end design and construction process. Unlike manufacturing, construction is a project based-production process. Lean construction is concerned with the holistic pursuit of concurrent and continuous improvements in all dimensions of the built and natural environment; design, construction, and activation, maintenance, salvaging, and recycling. This approach tries to manage and improve construction processes with minimum cost and maximum value by considering customer needs.

Lean construction is a "way to design production systems to minimize waste of materials, time, and effort in order to generate the maximum possible amount of value. Lean construction is about managing and improving the construction process to profitability deliver what the customer needs by eliminating waste in the construction flow due to construction contract, specification and agreement between client and other parties by using the right principle, resources and measure to deliver things right first time. The application of Lean production theory in construction is a complex process. This is because the adaptation of concepts and principles from manufacturing to construction is not straightforward. The meaning of concepts, principles and approaches used to explain and improve manufacturing processes must be well understood in order to transfer them to the construction environment. Furthermore, old thinking patterns must be abandoned in order to apply such concepts in the construction environment. Those patterns include the belief that construction industry is too particular to have any similarity with manufacturing as well as the focus on solutions exclusively drawn from new technologies and financial support when time and economic constraints are involved.

Undoubtedly, the implementation of Lean Construction theory and practice implies changes in organizations. It would require not only individual learning of new concepts and competencies, but also a change on the way things are done within organizations.

Lean construction is the practical application of Lean manufacturing principles, or Lean thinking, to the building environment.

Lean is about designing and operating the right process and having the right systems, resources and measures to deliver things right first time. Essential to this is the elimination of waste activities and processes that absorb resources but create no value. Waste can include mistakes, working out of sequence, redundant activity and movement, delayed or premature inputs, and products or services that don't meet customer needs.

Below are five key principles that need to be observed when Lean construction systems are designed. They are:

1. **Value**

Construction needs to adopt product focus that enables a long term dialogue to be started concerning the nature of value and how the product delivers it. The client requires a building to suit his purpose and provides value for money.

2. **Value stream**

The value stream identifies all those steps required to make a product. Identifying value stream, the way value is realised, establishes when and how decisions are to be made. The key technique behind value stream is process mapping for a very specific reason; that of understanding how value is built into the building product from client's point of view.

3. **Value stream maps**

This can be understood as processes flow charts that identify what action releases work to the next operation. Mapping brings choices to the surface and raises the possibility of maximising performance during construction.

At a strategic level, it offers a perspective on defining what is to be done. By taking this top down approach, the idea of identifying value streams such as the structure and the building envelope and considering how these systems are to be designed, supplied and constructed, offers a different way of organising for construction.
At a more tactical level, the value stream map can identify where waste lies in a particular process and this process

analysis shows how value stream can be achieved more effectively. A set of all the specific actions required bringing a specific product through:

    a. Problem solving task running from concept through detailed design and engineering to production launch.

    b. Information management task running from order taking through detailed scheduling to delivery.

    c. Physical transformation task proceeding from raw materials to finished products in the hands of the customer.

4. Flow

Flows are characterised by time, cost and value. Resources (labour, material and construction equipment) and information flows are the basic units of analysis in Lean construction. There are controllable and uncontrollable flows. Controllable flows such as materials or instructions from the warehouse or management respectively. Uncontrollable flows such as suppliers' provisions of resources and design information.

Strategically, flow is concerned with achieving a holistic route through the means by which a product is developed. It attacks the fragmentation that is inherent in the industry today by revealing it to be highly wasteful. Many have recognised this wastefulness and the leading solution is seen to be partnering.

Early stages of partnering are necessary prerequisites for improving construction. However, partnering remains only a partial solution. Lean works to eliminate places where value-adding work on material or information is interrupted. In construction, this may mean repackaging work so that parts of the project can proceed without completion of others and/or assure that resources are delivered in the order required and transported directly to the installation location to prevent double handling.

Construction problems are caused by negligence of flows. The construction process is seen as a set of activities; each is controlled and improved as such. Conventional managerial methods like Critical Path Method (CPM) deteriorate flows by violating principle of flow process, design and improvement. They concentrate on conversion activities. The resultant problem in construction tends to compound and self perpetuate. Under Lean thinking, improvement is possible by reducing uncertainties in workflow. Redesigning the planning system at the assignment level is the key to assuring reliable workflow and this step has to be implemented at a strategic level, pull identifies the real need to deliver the product to the customer as soon as he needs it. The traditional construction process pushes the client into an often-protracted development process where risk and uncertainties are prevalent.

5. Pull

The principle of pull suggests a decision where the ability to define quickly what the client needs from a building in relation to his business and subsequently customising and deliver them more predictably when the client requires them.

Three types of inventories need to be minimised:
        a. Material and design.

b. Labour and its tools.
c. Intermediate work product that has not been exploited.

Chapter 3: Integrated Project Delivery

What is it about a recession that makes collaboration look so appealing? That is not to say that collaboration is looked at negatively during strong market conditions; it's just the fact that when the economy is strong and jobs are moving forward, it's difficult for many AEC (architecture, engineering, and construction) professionals to make certain technological transitions that are necessary to streamline the collaborative process.

Conversely, a declining economy changes the landscape. With fewer jobs on the docket, and even less in the pipeline, companies are thrust into a situation where they need to squeeze every ounce of efficiency they can out of current practices. For many, though, this requires a new way of working, both internally and even externally with partners.

Throughout the past two decades, in particular, tougher conditions have generally accelerated the pace of technology adoption. One needs to look no further than the 1980s. Some would argue that it was during this time that slower market conditions spurred the transition from paper-based planning to CAD (computer-aided design) for many professionals in this industry.

Fast forward 20 years. Facing some of the toughest economic conditions in history, stakeholders in construction are once again looking for new ways to innovate. and for some, this means revisiting the age-old topic of collaboration. Only this time, rather than engaging in traditional means for collaboration, firms are instead looking at a new form of project delivery method called IPD (integrated project delivery). Then again, is IPD that new of a concept?

Old is New

Integrated project delivery is an approach to agreements and processes for design and construction, conceived to accommodate the intense intellectual collaboration that 21st century complex buildings require.

The inspiring vision of IPD is that of a seamless project team, not portioned by economic self interest of contractual silos of responsibility, but a collection of companies with a mutual responsibility to help one another meet an owner's goals. To support that vision, AEs, CMs, (architects/engineers, construction managers) and their lawyers are crafting management processes and contract terms intended to align the interests of the key project team with the project mission, increase efficiency, reduce waste, and make better buildings.

The main crux of IPD is around the idea of assembling all parties involved on a project as early as possible ideally during schematic design to provide a collective expertise to the development of a project before anything is designed. To incentivize parties, shared risk/shared reward contracts are established upfront with an understanding that all parties are working together for the good of the project.

An Industry veteran said "There is no technical reason why we cannot produce integrated drawings and there is no technical reason why we cannot build virtually before we build physically, the only thing that is standing in the way is this traditional contracting structure where everybody has these independent bodies and liability and insurance and traditional risk management policies."

IPD is a radical reordering of business relationships, the principal philosophical difference being that more traditional forms of project delivery typically establish adversarial relationships between contractors and design professionals, whereas IPD creates an environment of shared-risk/shared-reward for all principal project parties.

Shared risk/shared reward means that if a problem comes up on a project, the focus of the team is on finding a solution rather than assigning blame for the problem, so it instantly eliminates a lot of defensive documentation and changes the focus of the parties from protecting themselves to solving problems and getting the project done.

As little as few years ago we would have encountered either resistance or concern from people regarding IPD, due to some lack of awareness or understanding. Now, however, we sees a great deal of enthusiasm for and a strong desire to learn about how to make IPD work and we often wonders what factors have caused such a change.

Back before anyone had a computer there was nothing about the tools that would have prevented them from working in an IPD environment, but I have found myself wondering why now for IPD? Why did it take so long for us to figure this out?

Chapter 4: Last Planner System

While Lean construction's main tool for making design and construction processes more predictable is the Last Planner System (LPS) and derivatives of it, other Lean tools already proven in manufacturing have been adapted to the construction industry with equal success. These include: 5S, Kanban, Kaizen events, quick setup/changeover, Poka Yoke, visual control and 5 Whys.

The collaborative, commitment-based planning system that integrates should-can-will-did planning (pull planning, make-ready, look-ahead planning) with constraint analysis, weekly work planning based upon reliable promises, and learning based upon analysis of PPC (plan percent complete) and reasons for variance.

Users such as owners, clients or construction companies, can use LPS to achieve better performance in design and construction through increased schedule/programme predictability (i.e. work is completed as and when promised).

LPS is a system of inter-related elements, and full benefits come when all are implemented together. It is based on simple paper forms, so it can be administered using Post-it notes, paper, pencil, eraser and photocopier. A spreadsheet can help.

LPS begins with collaborative scheduling/programming engaging the main project suppliers from the start. Risk analysis ensures that float is built in where it will best protect programme integrity and predictability. Where appropriate the process can be used for programme compression too. In this way, one constructor took 6 weeks out of an 18-week programme for the construction of a 40 bed hotel. Benefits to the client are enormous.

Before work starts, team leaders make tasks ready so that when work should be done, it can be. Why put work into production if a pre-requisite is missing? This MakeReady process continues throughout the project.

There is a weekly work planning (WWP) meeting involving all the last planners design team leaders and/or trade supervisors on site. It is in everyone's interest to explore interdependencies between tasks and prevent colleagues from over-committing.

This weekly work planning processes is built around promises. The agreed programme defines when tasks should be done and acts as a request to the supplier to do that task. The last planners (that is the trade foremen on site or design team leaders in a design process) only promise once they have clarified the conditions of satisfaction and are clear that the task can be done.

Once the task is complete the last planner responsible declares completion so that site management or the next trade can assure themselves that it is complete to an appropriate standard.

A key measure of the success of the Last Planner system is PPC. This measures the Percentage of Promises Completed on time. As PPC increases; project productivity and profitability increase, with step changes at around 70% and 85%. This score is measured site-wide and displayed around the site. Weekly measures are used by the project and by individual suppliers as the basis for learning how to improve the predictability of the work programme and hence the PPC scores.

A key part of the continual improvement process is a study of the reasons why tasks promised in the WWP are delivered late.

Recording the reasons in a Pareto chart makes it easy to see where attention is most likely to yield the most results. Using tools like 5 Why analysis and cause-effect diagrams will help the team understand how they can improve the clarity of information and ensure that there are sufficient operatives.

Last Planner benefits don't stop at project predictability, profit and productivity; it contributes to positive changes in other industry KPIs. Research shows almost half the accidents and up to 70% less sickness absence on LPS managed sites.

Chapter 5: Lean Construction Eliminates Waiting

There is one process that is unusually successful in making the construction process efficient. "Lean a production management-based approach to project delivery" during the design-build construction timeline. Lean construction is renewing our work process from wasting materials, people, and time.

Lean's standards set up a process in which everything is thought through from an initial project planning meeting with everyone on board; the designers, the end users, the sub-contractors, the engineers, and other stakeholders. The idea is that if everyone openly communicates and discusses the objectives of the project, more problems can and will be solved earlier and quicker.

One good example from Lean is:

The hallway wall of a prison cell is typically pre-fabricated and set in place, then cement is poured, and much later doors are added. The problem is, if the cement is just a bit too high, the doors don't close. In one prison, fully a third of the doors had to be ground to fit. On a recent prison project, the management firm (at a Lean meeting) suggested that the wall pre-fabricator add the door to the pre-fabrication process. This was unheard-of, because it involved the coordination of two trades that did work in very different phases of the project. Upon investigation, the idea was found to be not only possible, but in the end it saved a large chunk of money.

Better still, the new approach is saving more money on each new project.

Now, this example is not a commercial workplace, but the Lean process can be applied to almost any project. Small and large projects.

One of the most well-known, large Lean projects is Terminal 5 at Heathrow Airport London United Kingdom.

Lean helps with everything from encouraging 1 shed of supplies instead of having subcontractors bring their own (they tend to break, or be forgotten more often with non-Lean projects) to keeping a gas pump at the site for installers to use instead of wasting time and money filling their own tanks at further and more expensive gas stations. Lean simply encourages the process of efficiency in each project.

Being able to meet with everyone on the team from the initial kickoff meeting throughout the project allows you to pull information out of everyone. By using straight forward computer visuals, the team is able to see the end project's technicalities. They can then predict exactly what each subcontractor will need. This eliminates waste and saves time and materials in the long run. As the previous example, some unexpected subcontractors are able to start their work off-site before installation, thereby saving even more time.

It takes the right mindset and attitude to take the Lean approach, but in the end, it is extremely rewarding. This process makes the entire team look at the end-goals and the big picture to figure out how to make the project, not necessarily by historical measures, but by what makes the most sense money and time based for that particular project.

The more Lean projects you do the more you learn about each role in the construction process and so the more efficient your time is spent. Meaning, generally speaking, the more projects you use Lean techniques with, the more profitable the projects can be. There is always continuous improvement.

Today, far too often we still are inundated with wasting time, energy, and money by having people waiting for materials and work waiting for people. Lean construction can organize collaboration and improve our work process efficiency. It is one step in the right direction.

Chapter 6: Performance Focused Lean Construction Application

We have discussed quite a few things in the previous chapters. We have learned that much of the quality Lean construction production management application and more importantly the results whether using Last Planner System or any other tools will be determined by the quality of the physical environment in which the day-to-day planning and communication activities occur. Some projects simply do not lend themselves to "big rooms" or large scale planning facilities. What we have learned is that there can be some common requirements to assure that the environment becomes a tool to facilitate shared definitions, shared vision and a shared understanding of production planning, production management and execution.

How exactly does being "Lean" apply to an average worker on a construction site? How does being "Lean" apply to a project manager's daily activities or even a design engineer on a design build project?

We have found that without a production Vision for a project or an organization that members (owners, architects, engineers, contractors, subs, etc) want to be "Lean" but struggle to see how that relates to what they do. We have adopted the belief to subordinate and synchronize all activities (Design, Engineering, Project Management, etc) to the desired rate, pace, route, sequence and flow of the project (represented by the work at the crew level) in order to achieve the production vision of Daily Crew Production Flow:

Every crew on every project effectively and efficiently completes their daily work assignment and specific production target free of incidents and defects while working within a safe, well prepared work area.

Our experience has been that agreeing to and communicating the Production Vision (Daily Crew Production Flow) creates a shared agreement and commitment between project participants as to what we are trying to accomplish on a daily basis with regard to Lean at the project level. Once a Production Vision for the organization or the project is agreed to, one can then begin to make the comparison between current conditions and the future state "Production Vision" of Daily Crew Production Flow.

We have had client organizations working with Construction and have challenged their crews to understand an abbreviated version "Production Pledge" (vs. the entire vision) so that the field understands their role in the journey to Daily Crew Production Flow.

Labels: Formal labels not only resolve ambiguity, they change outcomes. Labels craft the images that populate our thoughts; we are finding within our client organizations that the formalness of well printed labels begin to affect the behaviours of project teams in a positive manner. Bringing formality to the production planning facility seems to focus individuals in that environment on just that production planning. Labels also bridge the gap between mental models and theory to real world application. They create a common sense of obviousness and transparency between project participants from owner level to subcontractors and specialty trades. We have learned that they also facilitate the learning of "how to" when fulfilling production planning requirements (such as the requirement that Next Week's Production Plan be collaboratively planned and populated before the end of shift meeting on Friday afternoon). Labels depict the physical what and help with the how to.

Interactive – Simple – Plan Tables and Models: Production Planning is iterative and ongoing. Whether the project has 3 to 4 crews vs. 20 to 30 crews, whether it is a $3B project vs. $2.5M project, having a very simple, centrally located plan view of the product(s) or project phases can improve communication and coordination among crews using shared resources and shared work space. Simple planning tables and models are inexpensive simple communication tools that we have found aid in improved synchronization of crews, clarification of specific work areas and limits of work areas along with safety review and concerns associated with those areas.

Chapter 7: Collaboration and Lean Construction

The need for collaboration has been recognised in the UK and US construction industry for decades. Lean Construction has led to step changes in construction productivity using the principles of "Impeccable Coordination," "Projects as Production Systems," and "Projects as Collective Enterprise." Lean Construction practices lead to significant productivity improvements which have a positive effect on the bottom line.

So why was this Lean principles not adopted early in projects in the United Arab Emirates (UAE)?

The majority of contracts within the UAE construction industry are based on FIDIC (acronym for its French name Fédération Internationale Des Ingénieurs-Conseils) is an international standards organization for the construction industry.) FIDIC contracts have been used in the Middle East from the 1970s and familiarity appears to be the main reason for their continued use. This is despite the widespread belief that FIDIC contracts are thought to be too rigid, too adversarial and that they encourage a silo mentality that stifles collaboration.

The UAE construction industry needs to break with tradition and adopt other forms of contract that encourage Lean Construction.

Are there alternatives?

The US and the UK have both developed alternative forms of contract that encourage Conditions of Contract for Construction, which are recommended for building or engineering works designed by the Employer or by his representative, the Engineer. Under the usual arrangements for this type of contract, the Contractor constructs the works in accordance with a design provided by the Employer. However, the works may include some elements of Contractor-designed civil, mechanical, electrical and/or construction works.

Where to now?

The recent Building Smart ME report on the adoption of Building Information Modelling (BIM) in the Middle East found only 25% BIM usage in the industry. The full benefits of BIM applications can only be realised if there is collaboration amongst all parties involved in the building process. The UAE construction industry now has the tools in the form of Contracts and BIM applications to significantly improve the way they manage the design and construction of built environment.

The Bottom Line

It is difficult to see how an informed Developer will go any other way than Lean Construction route when procuring a new building. The danger for the industry is the familiarity with the FIDIC adversarial route, where everyone sit rather uncomfortably in their silos and don't collaborate.

Chapter 8: Three Lean Tools for Improving Construction Reliability

"Let me get this straight, you think we should reduce our inventory of cabinets? That is our safety buffer! What are we supposed to do when the hot glue machine breaks down again and we can't build cabinets, huh? We need buffer."

That was the reaction I got from a construction manager upon hearing my suggestion that he reduce his inventory of finished cabinets (this was on a construction project where the cabinets were being prefabricated nearby). His response was valid, but so was my suggestion.

From my perspective, I saw several problems with the excess inventory problems that are usually associated with this form of waste; finished cabinets were getting damaged as they sat around, they were often in the way of installers working in the building, and they were even creating a trip hazard for any passersby. It was not pretty.

From the perspective of the construction manager, he saw any reduction in cabinet inventory as a risk to the project schedule. His point was that if he eliminated his safety buffer, the unreliability of the cabinet-building process could cause cabinet production to halt, and potentially cause construction delays. Not only did the cabinet shop folks have problems with the hot glue machine, but they were also dealing with a whole host of other issues that created variation in process results; untrained cabinet builders, a messy workshop, conflicting production schedules, etc. Again, it was not pretty.

The Lean Approach

So, what to do? What would you, as a Lean thinker, do to create more reliability in the cabinet-building process? I have seen some practical Lean tools applied to construction processes that have yielded improved levels of process stability. Here are 3 of my favourite such tools:

1. 5S Visual Workplace

We all know about 5S by now, I am sure. It's a fantastic tool that can really help us create visual control of the workplace, so that we can spot abnormalities quickly. This would help reduce variation in the cabinet shop by reducing time wasted looking for tools and materials, as well as by eliminating the chance for a lost-time work accident by removing safety hazards from the workspace. This would no doubt help improve the stability of any construction process.

Construction Industry Particulars...

However, applying 5S to a construction site is a bit different than in a traditional workplace. The main difference is that construction projects are temporary in nature, while ongoing operations tend to be a little more permanent (although a wise strategy would be to design the workplace to be flexible enough to change with the times). This means that a 5S process designed for construction sites would need to be able to be implemented during a short ramp-up period, flexible enough to accommodate multiple stages of construction, and exceptionally easy to understand for those random people that tend to visit construction sites (inspectors, salespeople, etc.).

2. Preventive Maintenance

Just like factory workers depend on conveyor belts, press machines, and welding robots, construction workers depend on their ladders, generators, and hand-tools. Unlike Lean factory workers, most construction workers do not perform much preventive maintenance for their equipment. Often, equipment is just loaded up at the end of a long work day and tossed in the work truck. Worse yet, construction equipment is often exposed to Mother Nature in ways that most industrial equipment is not. This leads to a ton of equipment failures that slow down our construction processes, much like the hot glue machine did for our cabinet shop. A great approach for mitigating this source of variation is to implement basic Preventive Maintenance (PM) procedures.

Construction Industry Particulars...

PM is not a difficult concept to explain, but a frustratingly difficult tool to implement in the construction industry. This probably has more to do with bad habits than anything, so the big challenge is creating a work culture than encourages good habits. Instead of making it a habit to knock off work at the last second before the sun sets (which leaves little time for Preventive Maintenance), we should build-in time to inspect and repair our equipment. Instead of making it a habit to drag equipment on the ground, we should make sure that our people have better ways of transporting heavy items. Bad habits are hard to break, but the benefits of having reliable equipment far outweigh the costs of making a cultural change.

3. Job Instruction

Job Instruction (JI) is another great tool for improving process reliability. With construction processes, a lot of variation comes in the form of different techniques being used by different installers. Often, you can observe two installers building cabinets in four different ways. This is not good for consistency.

JI helps mitigate this source of variation by providing us with an effective approach to teaching standardized processes. Once we have established a set of best practices for cabinet building, we can incorporate them into a job sequence that can be taught using the Job Instruction method. This is a great tool for training new installers and cross-training veteran installers. By properly training our people, we can reduce variation between installers and greatly reduce the chance of human-related errors occurring.

Construction Industry Particulars...

The difficulty of implementing JI in the construction industry is that quite often the work is being done by sub-contractors who are not always amenable to being trained. Their business relies on having a reputation for knowing how to do good work, so nobody wants to submit to training, as that is an indication that they are still learning how to do good work. This is a huge cultural, systemic issue in the construction industry.

One way to overcome this barrier is to take the Toyota Way approach of investing in long-term suppliers. Choose sub-contractors who are open to long-term learning and partnership. Provide them with training on how to perform

JI, and let them become their own trainers. Work together to develop the standard job sequences that are being taught. Include JI as part of the statement of work for the contract. Think long-term.

The three tools listed above are just a few of the many available in a Lean construction manager's toolbox.

Chapter 9: 5S System on the Construction Job Site

Before real problem solving can begin... Before you can truly identify and eliminate waste... You must master 5S.

What is 5S?

Okay... don't let the text book definition scare you: "5S is a mnemonic for a workplace organization methodology that uses a list of five Japanese words which, translated into English, start with the letter S."

In other words, 5S is a method for organizing a work area, especially a shared work area (like a construction office or the jobsite), and keeping it organized. Done right, it will improve efficiency on your jobsite by eliminating waste, establishing work flow and reducing in-adherence to standards.

The 5S's on the Construction Jobsite

1. Sort

Going through all the boxes of materials, blue prints, permit boxes and driveway barricades in the construction office and keeping only what is essential. Do you really need those boxes of hardware? Does your inventory of permit boxes and driveway barricades exceed your planned starts for the next 9 months? What can you redistribute to another community that needs it, return to a Building Partner, or simply just throw away.

2. Set in Order

Focuses on efficiency. Don't confuse this with sorting or sweeping; the intent is to arrange any inventory or scraps left on the jobsite in a manner that promotes work flow. Is there a designated place for the left over rebar? Is there a standardized location for Homeowner colour kits? Clearly mark and label designated areas; whether it's a "broken and excess block area" on the jobsite or a shelf used only for colour kits. For everything there is place and everything should be in its place.

3. Sweep Daily

Systematic Cleaning or the need to keep the jobsite neat as well as safe. At the end of each day, the jobsite is straightened and any leftover materials placed in designated areas. This includes extra rebar, lumber, block, hurricane straps, AC duct work, and so on. Unusable materials must be placed in the dumpster. The key point is that maintaining cleanliness should be part of the daily work not an occasional activity initiated when things get too messy. Sweep daily doesn't mean on the third day when the Building Partner has completed his job; it means today and every day after that.

4. Standardize

Standardized work practices or operating in a consistent and predictable manner will eliminate innumerable sources of waste on your jobsite. If the Construction Professional is practicing 5S on the jobsite, every Building Partner knows exactly what his responsibilities are to sort, set in order and to sweep. So how does the Construction Professional achieve standardization? By reviewing Standardized Work Instruction

Sheets (SWIS sheets) with the crew, posting Hot Spot Sheets in the work area, marking reminders on FTQ inspection sheets, and talking to the crew when they are on the your jobsite.

5. Sustain the Discipline

Maintain and keep the standards you set, even when it's easier not to. There will be many times that you are going to want to simply look the other way. Don't do it. Once the previous 4S's have been established, they become the only way to operate on your jobsite. Maintain the focus, and do not allow a gradual decline back to the old habits. Hold your Building Partners accountable for completing the job (including your 5S system). But you must be disciplined as well.

Chapter 10: Steps to Sustaining the 5S System on the Jobsite

"Few weeks ago a Realtor/Estate Agent took some clients to one of our communities, where the couple noticed a difference in our home sites from other builders. The Realtor called me afterwards, describing our home sites as "immaculate" compared to other jobsites in the neighbourhood." (Construction Manager)

I mentioned this to the Construction Professional and he said, "Thanks. I have really been talking to the crews about sweeping and straightening before they leave." This is a huge first step.

While 5S does promote daily straighten and sweep, there is a key distinction between 5S and "standardized clean-up." The key concepts here are to improve work flow and to standardize so that anything out of order becomes obvious.

While one-on-one communication is critical, that alone will not sustain a 5S system on the jobsite unless you can physically be at every job, every day, to communicate your expectations to every crew.

Think of a 5S System as visual management over the jobsite. In other words, how can you get the jobsite to communicate your standards even when you are not there to explain them?

Step 1

Implement a labelling system. Post short, direct messages throughout the jobsite as both directions and reminders. One Construction Professional posts "BUILDING PARTNERS: PARK ON THIS SIDE OF THE STREET" bandit signs along the curb to control traffic flow, and "HARD HATS REQUIRED" signs beside each permit board.

HARD HAT

Another Construction Professional spray paints "SWEEP DAILY" on the slab floor as a visual reminder to his Building Partners to "leave the jobsite as neat as they found it."

Another Construction Professional painted signs directing Building Partners where to place unused rebar and other materials that will need to be returned or recycled.

Step 2

Post Hot Spot Sheets near the area where work will be performed. Your Building Partner will see it, and be reminded to pay extra attention to perform a task the right way. Eliminate recurring inspection failures, return trips to complete or redo work, and especially future warranty concerns.

One Construction Manager reviews Hot Spots daily before he begins his evening walk to check and lock houses. For each Building Partner who will perform work the next day, he prints the appropriate Hot Spot Sheets then tapes them near the area where the work will be performed.

Step 3

Communicate your expectations on the FTQ inspection sheets. If a Building Partner leaves the jobsite without straightening and sweeping; then it falls on you, the Construction Professional, to clean-up after him. But deduct points on the inspections sheet and write "Had to clean-up and sweep after the crew left" in the notes.

On the flip side, if a crew is good about following your 5S System, praise them both on the FTQ inspection sheet and with a phone call to the crew leader.

Your 5S System must follow each Building Partner through every activity in the building schedule. As a Construction Professional, you have got your work cut out for you and you will have to think strategically. Every activity presents its own set of challenges making 5S implementation difficult, and the temperament of your Building Partners to follow standards will change from day to day.

Understanding that holding your Building Partners accountable means that the buck stops with YOU, the Construction Professional. You have got to follow your 5S System before your Building Partner will.

Sustaining a 5S System on your jobsite won't happen overnight; but you can start today and, to achieve it, implant visual management. Be prepared to consistently remind and educate each crew about maintaining standards. The 5S System on the jobsite may begin with the Construction Professional, but the discipline is sustained through the Building Partner.

Chapter 11: Value Stream Maps

Value stream mapping (VSM) is a lean tool used to chart the flow of information and materials through the homebuilding system, from the beginning of a process to the end. In fact at Toyota, where the technique originated, it's known as "material and information flow mapping." VSM was pioneered by Toyota's chief engineer, Taiichi Ohno, and sensei Shigeo Shingo as a tool for productivity (as opposed to quality.) Because it's a simple visualization technique, it's especially effective in identifying burdensome, overly-complex systems (present state) and in designing simple replacements (future state).

By analyzing the value stream map, you can identify waste, design solutions and communicate lean concepts.

Creating a Value Stream Map

Step 1

Clearly identify the objective of the process.

Step 2

Identify all the positions (or people) involved in the process of achieving that objective. Cross-functional team members from construction, production, and sales to finance, IT, and design planning should be included in all mapping sessions.

Step 3

Write a step by step outline of each action in the process as information or materials is passed through each position.

Step 4

Draw a "current state" value stream map, which shows a step by step process flow. This is a flow chart diagram and must include all the steps as the process is currently conducted (not how it "should be" or "can be" conducted.) Show the good, the bad and the ugly. This is real world, as it happens today.

Step 5

Once the "current state" is mapped out, identify process times and delay times on actual steps or actions, as well as between actual steps and actions where no activity may be taking place. (This may be waiting times.) Make sure you have input from every position (or person) involved in the process.

Step 6

Next identify steps in the process that are non-value added. Another term for non-value added is waste. Waste is any activity that is not adding value to the end product or service. Target the 7 wastes specifically. (Often in homebuilding, non-value added is anything that the customer would be unwilling to pay for, but depending on the process, it can be anything that doesn't directly help you achieve the process objective.)

Step 7

Draw a "future state" value stream map that has eliminated or reduced areas identified as wasteful or non-value added. Again, this will be a flow chart diagram. Also, get input from every position (or person) involved in the process.

Step 8

Conduct a gap analysis. A gap analysis identifies the gaps (holes) between the current and future state. Develop counter measures to close the gap and implement the future state process.

The goal of a VSM is to clearly see (visually) the value in each step from the beginning of a process to the end. By creating a current and future state, you should weed out the non-value-added steps and further eliminate the 7 wastes.

Chapter 12: A3 Strategy Deployment

At its core, Strategy Deployment is an annual planning tool that sets a company's goals and targets, then develops a month-to-month improvement plan to get there. This plan lays out on an A3, which you could think of as your company's road map. This map shows us where we are today (What is actually happening) and where we want to go (What should be happening) and, ultimately, shows the planned route to get there.

Simplified, this road map provides

1. **Direction**

It defines your "True North," or the basic business needs that must be met. Obviously this includes cash generation, but would also tap into the very reasons your company is in business in the first place. Achieving these Targets is the sole purpose of Strategy Deployment.

2. **Determine the Gap**

You must know exactly where you stand if you are going to plot a course to your destination. Reflect on past success as well as those actions that failed to live up to expectation. Ask the hard question, "How close are you to achieving your Targets?" For example, your warranty expenses rose with increased tile cracks and you fell short of your sales goals which adversely impacted cash generation.

3. **Set Goals to Close the Gap**

   Your goals must be in-line with your True North. Reducing Warranty will improve Stakeholder Loyalty. Achieving Sales Budgets will increase Cash Generation.

4. **Write Specific Actions to Achieve the Goals**

   These Counter Measures are all the individual steps that you are going to take to achieve the goals. For example, you are going to
   1. Standardize tile installation.
   2. Implement a new tile underlayment to achieve your goal of reducing warranty, which will improve your Stakeholder Loyalty.

Obviously, we use the Strategy Deployment A3 as 10,000 foot view for annual goal setting and planning. This includes:
1. Enterprise Annual Strategy.
2. Local Building Company Annual Strategy.
3. Enterprise Advancement Team Annual Strategy.

Strategy Deployment can be broadened from an annual planning tool, to a road map for successfully implementing any improvement process. This includes:
1. A Strategy to Meet a Community Sales Budget.
2. Building Partner Performance Improvement.
3. Software Roll-out and Implementation.
4. Marketing Promotion.

Chapter 13: Construction-Sales Gemba Walks

Have you ever heard the joke about the New Home Sales Professional who went to Heaven?

A Sales Professional (SP) had a dream about arriving in Heaven and being greeted warmly by St. Peter. The SP toured Heaven to find beautiful tree-lined streets, with green, pristine conservation areas and all the best amenities such as a club house, Olympic sized swimming pool, separate bike and walking trails. Heaven was the perfect community. Then St. Peter pointed out the SP's new home, an 8,000 SF, 4-bedroom home with a freshly manicured lawn, blooming flowers and a sprawling old Oak tree.

A few weeks later, the SP was involved in an unfortunate car accident, was pronounced dead at the scene and end up back at the Pearly Gates. But this time things were different. Behind the gate waited neighbourhood streets lined with muddy tire tracks, vacant lots with knee-high weeds and wind-swept dirt piles, home sites littered with trash and construction debris. At the end of the street was the SP's new home, a run-down trailer with broken windows and an old, rusting refrigerator in the front yard.

The SP looked frantically at St. Peter and exclaimed, "What happened? This is a dirty, over grown neighbourhood. Just a few weeks ago there were clean beautiful streets and parks and a sparkling new home."

"Oh, I hadn't noticed," said St. Peter, shaking his head. "I'm here every day." This joke is about blinders and how we are all wearing them. When you are in the community, on the jobsite, in your model home day in and day out, you don't see all the little piles and clumps and growth that pops up. You are focused on all the countless activities within the building and selling process each one vying for your attention. That is why a dedicated, weekly Construction-Sales Gemba Walk is critical to the success of your community.

As you know, Gemba in Japanese means the place where all the activity is happening. Walking the Gemba together is part of "check" in Plan-Do-Check-Adjust (PDCA). It's the process of carefully observing to see where things are not as they should be.

So, for your weekly Construction-Sales Gemba Walk, take the blinders off and follow these steps.

1. Consistent day and time

Pick a consistent day and time that both the Construction Professional and the Sales Professional can walk the Gemba together. This is a standing appointment that is as important as keeping a Homeowner Meeting or any construction activity in the building schedule.

"I walk the community and model home with both of my Sales Professionals every Monday afternoon at 4:30pm," says one Construction Professional. "Both Sales Professionals are working on Mondays and Monday afternoons tend to be a little less hectic than the rest of the week."

Chapter 14: The 7 Wastes on the Construction Site

1. Waiting Waste

Also known as delay, waiting refers to the periods of inactivity that occur because a preceding activity didn't deliver on time or finish completely. Waiting waste increases cycle time during which no value-added activity is performed.

2. Motion Waste

This term refers to the extra steps taken by people to accommodate inefficient process layout, defects, reprocessing, overproduction or excess inventory. Motion takes time and adds no value to the product or service. To move and add value is called work. To move and not add value is called motion.

3. Over-processing Waste

This term generally refers to unnecessary steps in operations, such as reprocessing, double-handling, added communication and double-checking which adds no value to the product or service. Over-processing is often inserted into a process as a result of dealing with defects, overproduction or excess inventory.

4. Over Production Waste

Overproduction occurs when operations continue after they should have stopped. It's producing more than is needed, faster than needed or before it is needed. This results in product being produced in excess of what is required, products being made too early, and excess inventory carrying costs.

5. Transportation or Conveyance Waste

This is unnecessary motion or movement of products or materials that does not directly support immediate production, such as materials being transported from one jobsite to another or materials being transported from the jobsite back to the Building Partner. Ideally transport should be minimized for two reasons: It adds time to the process during which no value-added activity is being performed, and the material is exposed to handling damage.

6. Inventory Waste

This refers to any supply (materials or goods) in excess of what is required to build the current homes under construction. Inventory includes raw materials, work-in-process and finished goods. Though not all inventory is unnecessary waste, excess inventory can quickly build-up and tie-up cash and resources. All inventory requires additional handling and space.

7. Correction or Defects Waste

These are products, materials or services that do not meet expectation or conform to specification. Corrections and defects are anything not done correctly the first time and must be repaired, sorted, re-made or re-done, as well as materials which are scrapped due to defects.

Chapter 15: Examples of Motion Waste on the Jobsite

Motion is one of the 7 Types of Waste and honestly one of the most common examples of waste on jobsites. It refers to the extra steps taken by people to accommodate an inefficient process, defects, rework, reprocessing, overproduction or excess inventory. Motion takes time and adds no value to the product or service. To move and add value is called work. To move and not add value is called motion

Here are examples of motion waste on the jobsite as pointed out by a jobsite Construction Managers.

1. Jobsites and vacant lots get muddy and when Building Partners park in the mud, their trucks leave mud trails behind them. Construction Managers constantly have to sweep the streets to keep up curb appeal and to prevent debris from running into the sewers.

2. Show me a sewer cap buried under mulch in the landscaping and I will show you a frustrated Construction Manager who has to dig it out. It can take him 30 minutes just to find the sewer cap, and that is providing he notices the error before the inspector arrives. "We have failed more than one inspection because the sewer cap was buried and inaccessible" (Construction Manager).

3. How much time is wasted shuffling through an unorganized permit box? Anyone needing access (be it the Construction Manager, Building Partner or Inspector) has to open it slowly and very carefully or else all the paperwork will

spring out like a psychotic Jack-in-the Box. When this happens, the Construction Manager scrambles after paperwork blowing across the jobsite. On a good day, he is just digging into and fumbling through a crumpled mess.

4. This is the classic, text book example of not completing the job. When a crew leaves behind lunch trash, wrappers, cups, spit bottles, unused material, and miscellaneous scraps, someone is going to have to come in behind them and clean it up. Most often it is the Construction Manger, who can spend up to an hour at the end of the day straightening the jobsite. Sometimes it is the Sales Professional, who hurriedly scoops most things up into a single pile before a prospective buyer steps onto the home site. Sometimes it is the following Building Partner, who has to spend a good portion of his duration time sweeping before his crew can even begin and sometimes it is the Homeowners on either side of the jobsite, who have trash blown into their yard and bushes.

5. No one seems to respect the blue prints. They get left out in the sun and rain. They get walked over and trampled on. Trucks run over them. When the Construction Manager has to order a new set because the old one is undecipherable, there is another $45 down the drain…

6. Again, when a Building Partner doesn't fully complete his job, it is up to the next Building Partner to take time out of his schedule to finish it or worse, work around it.

7. Every Construction Manger in the company marked this scenario as an example of motion waste. After waiting all morning for the county inspector to arrive, the Construction Manager makes a quick trip to another jobsite. In his absence, the inspector arrives. It is Murphy's Law. If the Construction

Manager needed to speak to the Inspector, he is out of luck. If the Inspector needed to speak to the Construction Manager, the inspection is failed. It can and has on many occasions impacted cycle time. The recurring problem is so prevalent in fact; one Construction Professional addressed it in a recent Plan-Do-Check-Adjust project.

8. Motion waste runs rampant in an ineffective or inefficient process. In our system, we were experiencing a breakdown in Production providing a complete Start Packet to Construction when the job was released. There were a multitude of reasons for starting the job before the Start Packet was complete. Regardless, a start packet with missing documents causes the Construction Team headaches from cycle time delays, to frustrated Building Partners to failed inspections. Construction and Production are currently going through the Plan-Do-Check-Adjust cycle now to get to the root cause of the problem.

9. The Construction Manager has to check and recheck that there are no cuts or holes in the visqueen and it takes time to tape those holes shut again. That time wasted could be avoided if Building Partners walking across the slab would just watch where they step and if an accidental rip does occur, take the time to repair it themselves.

10. When a Building Partner crew fails to complete the job 100% the first time, the Construction Manager has to follow behind him, inspect the work, document the problem or defect, then call the crew supervisor, explain the problem and reschedule the crew back onto the jobsite. The Building Partner crew has to return to the jobsite and complete the job. Finally the Construction Manager re-checks the work,

and calls the crew supervisor to let him know the job was actually completed. Exactly how much motion waste is that?

11. One of our Construction Manager said, "You know, it is not like we are using invisible dog fencing. The silt fence is hard to miss." Still, those fences get run over, trampled and materials thrown on top of them like they are, well, not even there. They take a beating, and the Construction Manger has to take time every single day to put them back up, make repairs and, ultimately, pull them up and replace them. There is not only a motion waste involved, but a lot of dollars wasted replacing the material. Like the example before it, just watch your step… please.

Chapter 16: The Cost of Second Time Quality

In the closing process for most home builders, they provide a New Home Introduction (some call it an "Orientation" or "Walk Through") followed by a Re-walk Meeting. It is standard in the industry: the home buyers walk the home, put blue tape on defects, problems and corrections then the builder fixes everything and "re-walks" the home with the buyers before the closing. In fact, within the industry, builders expect the home buyer to find problems and even sets-up their New Home Introduction with the expectation that this is the buyer's opportunity to find corrections.

Why do home builder do that?

A lean homebuilder we use to work with will deliver the home 100% clean and complete at the New Home Introduction. In fact, to ensure the home is delivered at that standard, they have a 3rd Party Home Inspector walk the home to find any last minute touch-ups before they present it to the buyer. So, if the buyer finds defects, problems or corrections at the New Home Introduction, it should feel like a slap to the home builder ego. It is a blow to there reputation.

But it happens.

Sometimes, because there is a paint or drywall scuff. More often than not because they set the expectation that they are going to find defects. In fact, they are so certain of this, they actually pre-schedule a "Re-walk Meeting" at the same time they schedule the New Home Introduction. Have you ever heard of a self-fulfilling prophecy?

If you really believe in the quality of home you are delivering and the competency of the Construction Manager who built it, set the proper expectation for the New Home Introduction, then schedule it without prepping the Buyer to have to return to double check your work.

The cardinal rule of lean homebuilding is to complete the job right the first time. In other words, achieve First Time Quality. But we actually spend a great deal of time, resources and money achieving 2nd Time Quality. That is having to return to the jobsite to finish the job or fix an error. The money spent on 2nd Time Quality will nickel and dime the Building Partner's bottom line.

Most builders are astounded to discover the extent of costs dealing with quality issues embedded into normal construction processes. We tend to treat the constant stream of quality errors that plague daily operations as just another cost of doing business; that is, until we calculate the actual costs. We soon discover that the greatest profit opportunities may be inside our own organization.

Here are some recent examples of those hidden costs on the jobsite:

The cabinet installers didn't measure the back of the cabinets correctly for the plumbing, and there are now several large gaps around the plumbing penetrations into the wall. The Construction Professional had to call the cabinet company to return to the community to re-skin the cabinets.

The Cabinet Quality Assurance Supervisor spent 10 minutes on the phone with the Construction Professional then left his current job to drive out to the community to investigate the problem. The community was roughly 30 miles away and he spent 45 minutes talking to the Construction Professional onsite and inspecting the cabinets. He then spent 5 minutes on the phone with the Scheduler to go over the problem and to schedule the installer to correct the cabinets.

Meanwhile, the Scheduler spent five minutes on the phone with the Quality Assurance Supervisor, then an additional 15 minutes setting up the job. That included spending 10 minutes on the phone with the "Punch Guy" to explain the problem and give him directions.

Now the Punch Guy, an employee who is paid to return to jobs after the installer to complete or fix the work, has just spent 10 minutes on the phone with the Scheduler. He then drove out to the community, which was 15 miles from the shop and spent half an hour re-skinning the cabinets. He then called the Quality Assurance Supervisor and then the Scheduler to let them both know that he had finished and was returning to the shop.

Finally, at the end of the day, the Cabinet Quality Assurance Supervisor returned to the community to double check the Punch Guy's work. He just spent 5 minutes on the phone with the Punch Guy going over the rework. Now, from his last location, the community was 22 miles away, and he spent 20 minutes on the jobsite. When he finished, he returned to the shop 15 miles away and left a voice mail message for the Construction Professional that error had been fixed.

The Construction Professional called the electrical supervisor because the electrical crew left without installing all of the nail guards. He needed the crew back immediately to finish the job.

The electrical supervisor spent 7 minutes on the phone with the Construction Professional, and then another 10 minutes on the phone with the electrical crew leader. One person from the crew was going to have to go back to the community to finish the job.

The crew leader spent 10 minutes on the phone with the Supervisor then left his current job to return to the Construction Professional's jobsite. That community was just over 50 miles away. Once he got back to the jobsite, he found many nail guards missing, and spent half an hour finishing the job and walking the house with the Construction Professional.

The electrical company must also factor in the time lost from the paying job the crew leader was pulled from to complete the unfinished job for the Construction Professional.

The goal of 1st Time Quality is to eliminate 2nd Time Quality (or all those return trips). Quality-based cost reduction allows the Building Partner to recover hidden or buried costs and return that money to the bottom line.

Chapter 17: Construction Cost Reduction Starts on the Jobsite

Daily waste cost both the homebuilder and the Building Partner tens of thousands of dollars annually. The Construction Professional who firmly grasps this concept will position his community to leap out ahead of the competition. Those who manage their time and materials the best will elevate their company to become one of the top producers and most profitable builders in the market.

Unfortunately, waste runs rampant on the jobsite. Just today as I was walking some home sites I saw the dollars adding up. Not only was there a surplus of materials left over after a job was completed, but no one even tried to protect them from the rain.

On this one afternoon on this one home site alone, there was (conservatively) over $700 being thrown away with little thought to eliminating waste, much less simply reducing construction costs.

Now multiply this by the number of jobsites this superintendent was "managing." Then add the number of superintendents just like him in all the other communities, building homes on even more jobsites just like it. It is easy to see how the homebuilder and Building Partner lose tens of thousands of dollars annually needlessly to waste.

A Construction Professional uses lean concepts to give him the advantage over the competing builders. Lean will allow him to build faster with less error, which will naturally reduce construction costs. But to achieve this, he must pull those lean concepts out of the text books, beyond the classroom and onto his jobsite.

A Construction Professional engaged in lean transformation on his jobsite actively pursues and thinks about eliminating waste every day.

Forced Cost Reduction is not Waste Elimination

In the attempt to reduce construction costs, there will always be a tempting, easy, and immediate solution; require the trades, vendors and sub-contractors to reduce their pricing by a given percent. If they don't, replace them with a new company that offers cheaper pricing. This is called "Forced Cost Reduction."

Cost reduction is not the same as waste elimination. Forced Cost Reduction in fact violates the "partnership" between the Builder and the Trade, which is essential for both company's success. Partnership means eliminating waste together, so both the builder and the Trade benefits that is why we refer to our Trades and subcontractors as "Building Partners."

This partnership is successful when the Construction Professional and the Building Partner:
1. Go through standardized work instruction sheets and hot spots together.
2. Review First Time Quality notes together to eliminate delays and corrections, and improve jobsite readiness.
3. Commit to eliminating return trips, dry runs, and punch lists, together.
4. Walk material deliveries together to improve take-offs.

5. Walk homes under construction together to review blue print corrections and improvements.
6. Negotiate fair market pricing.

Cost reductions to competitively realign pricing with a down housing market is simply a reality of business. The cost of building the home can't go up when home prices are falling. But cutting a long term, quality Building Partner's pay by a few hundred dollars must be first measured against the number of opportunities to eliminate waste on the jobsite and, Forced Cost Reductions are never an acceptable answer.

A true Building Partner; as opposed to a trade, vendor or subcontractor deserves to be compensated a notch above fair market pricing however, a true Building Partner relentlessly pursues and eliminates waste on the jobsite and in the construction process alongside the Lean Construction Professional. A true Building Partner provides feedback for plan improvements and jobsite efficiency.

A Building Partner who is doing their part to proactively provide fair market value, manage material and process waste and communicates improvements to the home builder is earning a "top dollar" value within the organization.

Chapter 18: Kaizen and Plan-Do-Check-Adjust

So you have run into a problem, got an idea for an improvement or have identified waste in the system. What do you do next? Here is a guideline to follow when trying to decide whether to write an Idea Kaizen, a mini-PDCA or a PDCA B6.

Kaizen

Kaizen is a simple improvement. One-time or continuous, large or small, it aims to eliminate waste and rework, increase safety or improve quality. It is an action that you, personally, will take. Any idea that allows you to deliver on the promise of providing a pleasurable home buying, building and ownership experience is a Kaizen.

PDCA B6

When a problem occurs in the homebuilding system, we initiate a PDCA (Plan-Do-Check-Adjust), an iterative four-step problem-solving process. This problem-solving process follows the steps laid-out on the PDCA-B6. The B6 format includes a formal problem statement and goal statement, data collection (which graphically illustrates the problem then breaks it down to a Point of Cause). It also includes problem investigation, which includes brain storming, a fishbone and 5-Why analysis mining down to several root causes. There are counter measures with set target dates to implement, and follow-up which shows if the counter measures succeeded in eliminating the root causes.

A strong PDCA group includes 4 to 6 people, and every position affected by the problem must be represented. This includes multiple positions within the organization, as well as Building Partners, Market Partners and other stake holders.

Examples:

When 50% of the homes in a six month period required the painter to return to complete interior window caulking, two Construction Professionals initiated a PDCA B6 with the QI inspector and the painter.

When 30% of the Sales Professionals were not using the online pricing memorandum to reference community pricing guidelines, two company presidents, the IT programmer and the Director of Finance initiated a PDCA B6.

Mini-PDCA

The mini-PDCA is a hybrid of the PDCA and Kaizen. It is a watered down version of the PDCA B6 that was designed to be filled-out quickly and efficiently on the Gemba. It follows the Plan-Do-Check-Adjust format, providing space for a problem and goal statement, a point of cause, root causes and counter measures. It walks you through the steps but sacrifices data collection and problem analysis, including the fishbone and 5-Why.

The Mini-PDCA includes a group of two to four people and are most often used for initial problem investigation, or when a great deal of problem investigation and data collection would seem like overkill. But don't use the Mini-PDCA as an excuse to mountain jump; you should never approach any

PDCA with the root causes or counter measures already determined.

Warning: The mini-PDCA format should be used sparingly, as depending on the problem and analysis, it can make the statement, "We only spent 10 minutes on this."

Examples:

A Construction Professional worked a mini-PDCA with a Building Partner who consistently missed turning-in FTQ inspection sheets and devised a counter measure to help his crew complete and turn-in the sheets on the jobsite.

A Production Planner worked a mini-PDCA with two Construction Professionals who consistently emailed vague or incomplete take-off information to her.

A Sales Professional worked a mini-PDCA with the printer/graphic artist when the design of an inventory flyer wasn't producing the expected number of inquiries.

A New Strategy for the Kaizen Blitz

We have initiated a Kaizen Blitz several times this year to collect information for PDCAs. In the past, the leader of a PDCA group casually emailed a question to Teammates. The responding Kaizens, generally, were a few sentences describing a possible counter measure.

For a construction PDCA initiated last week, the group leader and I decided to hit the pause button and examine our Kaizen Blitz process more closely.

This PDCA is looking into a recurring waste in which jobsite blue prints are replaced at least once if not multiple times during the construction of the home. This is costing them roughly $45 per replacement and the PDCA group wants to initiate a Kaizen Blitz to collect infomation about the recurrence of this problem across all communities.

That brought us to the purpose of a Kaizen Blitz. The PDCA group first had to define their objectives:

a) How many other communities are experiencing this waste and what are the details?

b) Are communities that are not experiencing this problem doing something that the others aren't?

So our experiment began with the PDCA group setting up a Kaizen for every member of the Construction Team. In this Kaizen, the problem description was clear and concise and included a photograph of a wet, tattered set of blue prints that would now have to be thrown away. (That's $45 in the trash, and another $45 for a new set of prints.)

Rather than a casual email, the PDCA group gave the Construction Team information to build a worthwhile Kaizen. Next the PDCA group leader wanted to ensure the Construction Team understood the group's expectations.

He said he wanted each Construction Professional to put some thought into what they see in their environment, then write a thought-out explanation for causes and counter measures. That led us to the next step.

In the Kaizen we set-up for the Construction Team, the PDCA group pre-set questions in the root cause and counter measure fields. For the root cause, they asked the Construction Professional to fill-in the "why, where and who." Then in the counter measure field, they asked, "What have you done to prevent this and did it work?"

Some Construction Professionals may only be able to answer one section and not the other. That is okay. If a community is experiencing blue print re-order waste, the Construction Professional should be able to point where and why he sees it happening, even if he is not sure what to do about it. Another community that isn't experiencing this waste may be taking preventative steps without fully realizing why. ("If it ain't broke, don't fix it.")

Finally, this Kaizen Blitz should achieve something that no other blitz has managed to achieve: 100% participation. Past Kaizen Blitz have always had strong participation, but generally if a Construction Professional does not have that problem in his community or has no ideas for a counter measure even if he is experiencing the problem; he does not participate in the Kaizen Blitz.

Because this PDCA group set-up a Kaizen for every member of the Construction Team and set clear expectations, they are expecting feedback from 100% of the team.

Chapter 19: Creating the Fishbone and 5-Why Analysis

The 5 Why Analysis is a question-asking exercise used to explore the cause/effect relationships underlying a particular problem. Ultimately, the goal of applying the 5 Why method is to determine the Root Cause of a defect or problem. The Fishbone is a diagram that illustrates the thought process behind the 5 Why Analysis. It shows the Point of Cause in the "head" of the fishbone, the Affinity Statements as the first why of each "rib" or "leg," and a drill down of WHY? phrases (preferably 5) for each Affinity Statement.

Step 1

Set-up the Fishbone Diagram by writing the Point of Cause (POC) in the triangular head of the fishbone.

Step 2

List each Affinity Statement along the body of the fishbone. This statement is your first "why?" so write each Affinity Statement as if answering why it is contributing to the POC. Include a noun and verb in the statement. A single word answer is not acceptable; it will confuse someone reviewing the PDCA.

Step 3

Now begin the 5 Why Process. For the first Affinity Statement, ask, "why?" at least four more times. Keep your answers as simple as possible, as if you are talking to a child.

The Why? answers must be clear, concise phrases that include a noun and a verb. It is critical that the PDCA group drills deep - ask "Why?" at least four more times, if not more.

Step 4

Sometime, you have two answers to a why question. Show both answers on the fishbone by making a fork that leads the answers into two separate directions. Then continue asking "why?" in both directions.

Although the "five" in 5 Whys is not gospel, it is held that five iterations of asking why is generally sufficient to get to a root cause. Fewer than five and the risk of missing the root cause increases. The real key is to encourage the PDCA group to avoid assumptions and logic traps and instead trace the chain of causality to a root cause that still has some direct connection to the problem statement.

Step 5

Once you have answered the 5 Whys for each leg of the fishbone, circle the root causes. Do not choose more than 4 root causes within one PDCA. Keep it simple. Also, the root cause will always be an end or final why on the leg. It cannot be a preceding why.

Step 6

Work the Therefore Test. Double check that the chain of causality makes sense, and that it is not missing a Why statement. To do this, begin with the Root Cause (or the final Why) and work backwards saying "therefore" between each answer. This process will often make a missing Why? stick out like a sore thumb.

Chapter 20: Applying Lean Thinking in Construction

As we pointed out in previous chapter; Lean construction is a philosophy based on the concepts of Lean manufacturing. It is about managing and improving the construction process to profitably deliver what the customer needs; because it is a philosophy, Lean construction can be pursued through a number of different approaches.

This chapter will outlines the elements of Lean manufacturing and suggests how these might be adapted to deliver Lean construction in practice.

Lean manufacturing was initially pioneered and developed by the large Japanese car manufacturers. It has been implemented by a number of Japanese, American and European manufacturers with considerable success, and has been widely applied outside the automotive industry.

Lean is about designing and operating the right process and having the right systems, resources and measures to deliver things right first time. Essential to this is the elimination of waste activities and processes that absorb resources but create no value. Waste can include mistakes, working out of sequence, redundant activity and movement, delayed or premature inputs, and products or services that don't meet customer needs.

The primary focus is on moving closer and closer to providing a product that customers really want, by understanding the process, identifying the waste within it, and eliminating it step by step.

Production and management principles

Lean is focused on value, more than on cost, and seeks to remove all non-value adding components and (especially) processes whilst improving those that add value. It aims to define value in customer terms, identifying key points in the development and production process where that value can be added or enhanced. The goal is a seamless integrated process (value stream) wherein products 'flow' from one value-adding step to another, all driven by the 'pull' of the customer.

The idea of 'right first time' is essential to the Lean philosophy. 'Right' in this context means making it so that it can't go wrong. This approach involves an extremely rigorous, questioning analysis of every detail of product development and production, seeking continuously to establish the ultimate source of problems. Only by eliminating the cause at source can the possibility of that fault recurring be removed.

Design and product development

Lean manufacturers have developed systems for product development which first identify the right product (in terms of customer needs), and then design it correctly so that it can be manufactured efficiently. 'Design', in manufacturing terms, is concerned with the development and integration of systems and components into coherent, efficient and buildable products, not just the styling of the exterior appearance, a task which is often undertaken by external agencies.

Tools have been developed to capture and analyse customer perceptions and requirements for product quality and performance. These tools also enable product development and manufacturing performance targets to be established. Design development targets include reductions in design changes and process iterations.

Lean Production

Lean manufacturers arrange production in closely located 'cells' so that work flows continuously, with each step adding more value to the product. The standard time for all activities is known and the objective is to totally eliminate all stoppages in the entire production process. However, only optimum stocks of material are kept as buffers between processing stages.

For this system to be effective, every machine and worker must be completely capable of producing repeatable perfect quality output at the exact time required. Workers are responsible for checking quality as the product is assembled, and in some instances given authority to stop production if defects arise. In this way, quality problems are exposed and rectified as soon as they occur.

The workforce is kept informed of progress towards their production and cost targets by use of information displays so that everyone is able to see the status of all operations at all times. Work teams in Lean manufacturing are highly trained and multi-skilled, and many of the traditional supervisory and managerial functions have been devolved to them.

Supply chain management and supplier relationships

Lean manufacturing is based on the elimination of waste, including time lost waiting for missed/delayed supplies, unnecessary storage and the value tied-up in large stocks of parts waiting for assembly. 'Just in time' (JIT) delivery is therefore a vital element, and to deliver this Lean manufacturers have had to develop their network of suppliers. Significant efforts are applied to encourage them to adopt the same Lean manufacturing principles and systems, often company-wide, rather than solely related to that part of the suppliers' operations that affect the manufacturer.

Lean manufacturers have moved away from traditional relationships with their suppliers to partnering arrangements with a smaller number based on good communications and open-book accounting. These relationships work by both parties sharing philosophies of continuous improvement (especially in the area of defect reduction, cost and timeliness of delivery) and sharing business and development strategies sufficient for both parties to know enough about each other to make forward planning effective.

Applying Lean thinking to construction

The Lean principles can only be applied fully and effectively in construction by focusing on improving the whole process. This means all parties have to be committed, involved, and work to overcome obstacles that may arise from traditional contractual arrangements.

Design

   a. Use of visualisation techniques such as Virtual Reality and 3D CAD to fully define the product requirements from the customer's perspective.
   b. Value Management to achieve more understanding and focus on client value.

    c. Use of integrated design and build arrangements (including partnering) to encourage close co-operation between designers, constructors and specialist suppliers.
    d. Design for Standardisation and Pre-assembly – both of components and processes to achieve higher quality, time and cost savings.

Procurement

    a. Supply chain management and rationalisation of the supply chain to integrate all parties who contribute to the overall customer value into a seamless integrated process.
    b. Transparency of costs - the elimination of waste in both processes and activities requires a clear and complete understanding of costs to ensure decisions on customer value can be taken.
    c. Confidentiality of cost and cash flows must be addressed.
    d. The concept of partnering, all involved parties contributing to a common goal with the boundaries between companies becoming less critical.

Production Planning

    a. Benchmarking to establish 'best in class' production methods and outputs.
    b. Establishment of a stable project programme, with clear identification of critical path.
    c. Risk management - to manage risks throughout the project

Logistics

    a. Just-in-time delivery of materials to the point of use eliminates the need for on-site storage and double-handling

Construction

    a. Clear communication of project plans.
    b. Training, teamwork, multi-skilling.
    c. Daily progress reporting and improvement meetings.
    d. A well motivated, well trained, flexible and fully engaged workforce.

Example 1

A Local Contracting in England, a specialist cladding and roofing contractor, have used the principles of Lean thinking to increase their annual turnover by 20% in 18 months with the same number of staff. The key to this success was improvement of the design and procurement processes in order to facilitate construction on site, investing in the front end of projects to reduce costs and construction times.

They identified two major problems to achieving flow in the whole construction process – inefficient supply of materials which prevented site operations from flowing smoothly, and poor design information from the prime contractor, which frequently resulted in a large amount of redesign work.

To tackle these problems our local Contracting combined more efficient use of technology with tools for improving planning of construction processes. They use a computerised 3D design system to provide a better, faster method of redesign that leads to better construction information. Their design system provides a range of benefits, including isometric drawings of components and interfaces, fit co-ordination, planning of construction methods, motivation of work crews through visualisation, first run tests of construction sequences and virtual walk through of the product. They also use a process planning tool known as Last Planner, to improve the flow of work on site through reducing constraints such as lack of materials or labour.

Example 2

A design and build firm, is one of the most successful and fastest growing construction companies in UK. The firm has worked to understand the principles of Lean thinking and look for applications to its business, using 'Study Action Teams' of employees to rethink the way they work. They have reduced project times and costs by up to 30%, through developments such as:
  a. Improving the flow of work on site by defining units of production and using tools such as visual control of processes.
  b. Using dedicated design teams working exclusively on one design from beginning to end and developing a tool known as 'Schematic Design in a Day' to dramatically speed up the design process.
  c. Innovating in design and assembly, for example through the use of pre-fabricated brick infill panels manufactured off site and pre-assembled atrium roofs lifted into place.
  d. Supporting sub-contractors in developing tools for improving processes

Chapter 21: Lean Construction Supply Chain

Construction is one of the major industries throughout the world, accounting for a large proportion of most countries' Gross Domestic Product (GDP). Moreover, the importance of the construction sector is not only related to its size but also to its role in countries' economic development. It produces the facilities that house a wide variety of human activities, as well as the infrastructure that connects these facilities into an increasingly complex network.

Although today construction industry has made great strides technologically and management wise throughout the world, these developments have not led to the adoption of the Supply Chain Management systems. The application of Supply Chain Management (SCM) techniques have been yielding successful results in various industries for decades. As is known, Supply Chain comprises all the logistics activities associated with processing the physical flows; from sourcing and transporting raw materials, to delivery of the finished product to the end customer.

The benefits of implementing SCM are numerous e.g. cost reductions along the supply chain, increased supply chain surplus, better communication and information sharing between partners, agility, responsiveness ,and increased customer satisfaction to name but a few. Adaptation of SC processes into the construction industry is a pressing need in today's competitive environment and has a vast potential to increase effectiveness and efficiencies in all activities of construction industry such as production, procurement, logistics and collaboration with subcontractors.

Findings emanating from investigations have been critical of the construction industry's fragmented nature, lack of coordination and communication between participants, adversarial contractual relationships, lack of a customer-supplier focus, price based selection, and ineffective use of technology. The same as in most sectors the demands of the construction industry clients are increasingly growing; lower cost, faster and more responsive construction processes, shorter execution durations, more reliable work schedules and higher-quality facilities (buildings) are required and demanded in the construction industry.

These demands generally involve more responsive building design, production and closer coordination between the clients and the constructors. Construction Supply Chain Management programs could be very effective panacea to tap these kind of demands. Therefore the more effective Construction Supply Chain Management (CSCM), the more effective construction project executions. CSCM is recently emerging area of practice which is inspired from Manufacturing Supply Chain Management but differs substantially in some respects. It is a comprehensive and holistic concept that is mostly concerned with the coordination of discrete quantities of thousands of materials delivered to specific construction projects. As mentioned before, Construction industry has a highly fragmented nature and it consists of a plethora of companies.

There is lack of communication and problems in maintaining relationships among members of construction industry (contractors, subcontractors, suppliers, clients etc.) along the supply chain. Such fragmentations lead to delays and complexities, thereby create disputes among supply chain members and cost increases, all of which result in grave inefficiencies in the construction industry. Commonsense indicates that it is wise to form Construction Supply Chains (CSCs) in order to cope up with the serious problems of construction industry. As a matter of fact, many experts have suggested creating CSCs as a potential solution to eliminate these kinds of inefficiencies and to reap the fruits of an integrated and efficient supply chain.

Adaptation of SCM to the Construction Industry Operations

It is only recently, precisely during 1990s, the importance of SCM in improving the performance of building projects has been started to be recognized. Traditionally construction industry has been organized along the lines of outsourcing. In this respect, the construction contractors and subcontractors have usually displayed opportunistic behaviours to compensate and recover from unacceptably low tendered profit margins. Unfortunately most of the construction industry firms did not perceive the drawbacks and disadvantages of this approach.

Construction Supply Chain Management (CSCM) is a specialized variant of SCM which is designed for unique characteristics of construction industry. SCM in construction (CSCM) can be defined "the network of facilities and activities that provide customer and economic value to the functions of design development, contract management, service and material procurement, materials manufacture and delivery, and facilities management. Construction Supply Chains are typically make-to-order supply chains, every project is unique and with every project a new product is created. As compared to other sectors, the fragmentation of the construction operations (particularly procurement) in traditional construction industry have proven to be relatively unsophisticated as far as supply chain applications are concerned. This is where the modern, integrative and holistic supply chain management programs should be stepping in to find solutions for the problems created by the fragmentation of the construction process. It is only with this kind of SCM programs the various dimensions of the programs could be integrated. Meanwhile, the importance of information transactions should not be overlooked in CSCM; because CSCM is essentially a process of information transaction. Therefore, it will be wise to treat information as a resource in CSCM projects

Since construction process has a fragmented nature, it leads to inefficient division of labour. Construction supply-chain management offers new approaches to reduce the cost and increase the reliability and speed of facility construction. It also offers a way to work that can fulfill the promise of a cooperative and collaborative construction environment. The promise of supply-chain management comes from its system perspective on production activities. Logistics cost, lead time and inventory has a large share in supply chain. Therefore focusing on CSCM is fully appropriate in construction industry. The focus may be particularly on the impact of the supply chain on site activities in order to reduce site costs and duration. Here, the primary consideration is to ensure material (and labour) flows to the site for the sake of avoiding disturbances in the workflow. Furthermore the focus may extend on transferring activities from the site to upstream stages of the supply chain. The rationale may simply be to avoid the inferior conditions of site, or to achieve wider concurrency between activities, which is not possible in site construction with its many technical dependencies.

Due to both global sourcing of materials and assemblies, shortage of craft labour, value-added work to be conducted off-site CSCM receives more emphasis than before. In all types of businesses and supply chain operations uncertainty is a fact of life. Uncertainty affecting Supply Chain operations has long been recognized by researchers as a major obstacle to the delivery of customer value in Supply Chains therefore elimination of uncertainty particularly in the construction projects is utmost concern. As a matter of fact, CSCM programs are adopted to cope up with uncertainty. Much of the uncertainty arises out of a lack of visibility and awareness throughout the construction supply network; because of this accumulation of material, buffers are commonly perceived within the construction industry as an effective means of shielding a project from the risks associated with uncertainty in the supply network. To cope up with the problems of traditional approach, Automated Materials Locating and Tracking Technologies (AMLTT) is brought up to improve construction Supply Chain visibility and reduce uncertainty.

Chapter 22: Lean Construction Waste Management

Lean construction is the practical application of lean manufacturing principles, or lean thinking, to the building environment. Engineers, constructors, and consultants who are shaping this concept envision a project as a production system.

Although there are volumes written about lean manufacturing from many viewpoints, lean construction literature and consulting offerings are both generally aimed in the direction of the general contractor. This chapter explores how lean construction can eliminate waste in the erection of plumbing and mechanical systems that are prevalent in coal, gas, or nuclear power plant construction.

Lean Construction: Here and Now

There has been a notable increase in the popularity of lean construction in the general construction industry especially in the past years as a result of at least two main drivers. First, plant managers seeking to reduce their total cost of ownership and mitigate the effects of unforeseen risks consider lean construction as a new execution platform. Second, energy-oriented construction firms looking for ways to be more competitive in the wake of the 2008 U.S. economic crisis are attracted to lean construction as a new model for conducting business. The application of lean thinking concepts has produced success stories in several construction segments, most notably in health care construction.

Unfortunately, marketplace confusion persists around how lean construction can be used to improve efficiency or even reduce costs of a highly engineered and complex construction project such as a power plant retrofit. Part of this confusion is due to the relative newness of the concept of lean construction, which has been spurred on by an approach marketed as the "Last Planner System" (LPS). Although LPS and LPS-like systems incorporate basic lean thinking principles, the dimensional focus of these systems is on the project; that is, LPS and LPS-like systems purposefully focus on the activities occurring in the field and pay only minor attention to the rest of the supply chain activities like subcontractor shops and supplier facilities.

Mechanical contractors engaged in the energy industry can easily misinterpret the benefits of LPS and LPS-like systems as the single most important element in a lean transformation for their company. That is, by implementing an LPS or LPS-like system, a trade contractor company may mistakenly believe that it is a lean organization. However, LPS and LPS-like systems are but a single portion of a lean construction transformation.

Let's explore how lean construction relates to a piping and mechanical contractor that is building a complex copper piping system for a gas-fired power plant, at three distinct levels; the firm, the project, and the program level.

Three Levels of Lean Construction

We propose a hypothetical construction project structure involving a mechanical contractor, an electrical contractor, a structural contractor, a general contractor (GC), a plant manager, and an architect/engineer (AE) to illustrate the three levels of lean construction.

For simplification, the plant manager decided that the project will use a GC approach to project delivery as opposed to one with a design-build approach. In the traditional execution of this project, first the AE issues construction drawings to the plant's engineering and construction representative. Then the plant submits a request for proposal against the scope of the job to one or several qualified GCs, and, in turn, the GC does the same to several qualified subcontractors.

Lean Implementation at the Firm Level

From the perspective of the mechanical contractor in this example, that group has expertise in a number of cash conversion processes, referred to by the staff as "copper" or "steel," which serve the needs of all of its power plant customers. These processes include all elements of design/coordination, procurement, fabrication, and installation.

1. Meeting the customer's needs. From the perspective of the contractor, copper piping is seen as a production system with inputs and outputs. These processes include all elements of design/coordination, procurement, fabrication, and installation.

The size of the plant project and sophistication of the mechanical firm may dictate that the design, procurement, and fabrication steps of the production system occur away from the plant site in the contractor's regional office or fabrication shop. The intermediate product, in this case copper spools, is transferred to the plant site for efficient final installation. Often, these steps are manually coordinated and use disparate tracking systems.

This fragmented production system is manageable for a low-volume mechanical firm, but as the demand for services increases, system inefficiencies will magnify operational constraints and increase inventories. For example, the mechanical contractor often manages several projects within a region for multiple power plant customers and may manage several projects at a single power plant. The contractor also operates a single regional fabrication shop and maintains a design and coordination staff. Each project has different customers, scheduling demands, and business priorities. This complexity highlights the inherent inefficiencies in the design-engineering-fabrication process and causes increased variability.

Consider the scenario where a contractor is hanging pipe for three different projects for three different customers in parallel. The contractor may decide to improve consistency in operations through continual improvement in one or more "cash-to-pipe" conversion processes that are the same, regardless of the customer or project.

2. A belt-tightening approach. Lean thinking at the firm level focuses on continual improvement in one or more cash conversion processes, such as "copper piping" for a mechanical contractor, which involves all of the core competencies of design, procurement, fabrication, and installation. This process is consistently applied over and over for multiple clients and multiple projects.

The following are some examples of lean implementation at the firm level:

a. Evaluate and implement an appropriate balance between pull and push in the production model.
b. Reorganize the fabrication shop systems to improve material flow.
c. Develop an integrated process that eliminates or reduces the effects of the often troublesome handoff from design to procurement to fabrication.

These activities are wholly within the control of the contractor. Therefore, when operating from this perspective, the project manager or superintendent for the mechanical contractor makes daily decisions that generally result in improved overall performance for the mechanical contractor's business. That person may decide to use the strategy of a constant stream of installation rates, which provides a consistent flow and demand for the design-procurement-fabrication process. This, however, may cause deficiencies (such as not keeping up with the schedule) or excess supply (such as working too far ahead) at the project level from the GC or owner's perspective.

Lean Implementation at the Project Level

At the project level, the mechanical contractor is one of several trade contractors involved in a project. The project is a temporarily formed organizational structure or supply chain with a defined start and finish. As expected, the plant manager or GC would drive the requirement to deliver the project using lean techniques.

3. Plant construction project as a production system.

From the perspective of the plant manager, the project is depicted here as a production system with inputs and outputs. The production system in the middle of this diagram is the set of processes that drive all activity toward completing a given project. The production system in the middle of this diagram is the set of processes that drive all activity toward completing a given project. This production system involves multiple firms and their unique processes, such as copper, steel, underground work, or glazing. In the hypothetical project structure, the design, engineering, and procurement steps for the mechanical, electrical, and structural contractors may still occur in remote offices or project trailers, while the construction and installation effort is, by necessity, field-centric.

Today's waste reduction and productivity efforts for the project purposefully focus on improving the flow of work on a single capital construction effort through the implementation of lean thinking concepts in the field. The project level does not necessarily concern itself with ensuring that the individual businesses that provide construction services are operating efficiently, but rather focuses on determining how all of the construct/install steps for each trade can be done efficiently.

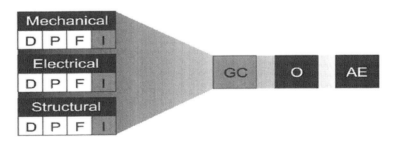

Notes: D = design activities, P = procurement activities, F = fabrication activities, I = installation activities, GC = general contractor, O = owner or plant manager, AE= architect/engineer.

4. Improved management in the field. This diagram depicts lean thinking focused on the project activities that occur in the field. Some lean techniques that are applied in the shaded zone include early contractor involvement in design, multi-tiered and integrated planning, and tracking of field commitments between and among all parties.

The lean techniques in the shaded zone in the diagram involve several facets. Among them are early contractor involvement in design, multi-tiered and integrated planning, and tracking of field commitments between and among all parties. Though it is beyond the scope of this chapter, field productivity at the plant site is a major emphasis of LPS and LPS-like systems. In practice and theory, the mechanical trade installs its pipe spools in a manner that will not conflict with the electrical or structure trades and will make tradeoffs to ensure seamless integration of the build process on the plant site.

In theory, project managers or superintendents for the mechanical contractor at the project level, in harmony with the overall plant construction project team, make daily decisions that result in improved overall performance for the project. This is significantly different from the concepts discussed from the firm's perspective. The project-oriented lean solution may conflict with a trade contractor's desire to reduce working capital required for the whole firm that is balancing supply and demand of piping spools for multiple projects and customers.

Consider how the copper pipe production system works at the project level. Any delay in receiving prefabricated spools at the plant site could cause negative consequences and personal commitments to go unmet, perhaps affecting plant start-up. Foreseeing a problem, a wise superintendent might order extra spools from the fabrication shop each week more than could possibly be installed given the constraints they face. This action causes the bullwhip effect, where the demand requirements are amplified as you move upstream in the process where there is less certainty concerning the information related to project demands.

In extreme scenarios, the fabrication shop could easily become cluttered with supply of prefabricated spools as an insurance policy. The problem is that this inventory of in-process material represents tied up working capital, and much of this takes place out of sight of the plant construction effort.

Toyota discovered that having only an efficient assembly line was an isolated way of thinking, because this forced waste or inventory further upstream to suppliers, which drove up total costs. In the case of power plant construction, some of the waste from using popular field-based lean techniques is shifted to the trade contractor's fabrication shops and even further upstream to the design and procurement offices. The lowest cost of construction will not fully materialize in this case.

For these reasons, a combination of the lean firm perspective and lean project approach is needed to create a holistic lean solution that will transform the industry of constructing power plants.

Lean Implementation at the Program Level

At the program level, the plant has a predefined amount of capital work to accomplish in a given time frame, which could be one year or five years. The sophisticated plant manager has taken the time to organize the work into buckets whereby some of the work is bid and other work is negotiated. In some cases, the negotiated work scope is made visible early to service providers to allow for integrated resource planning. Most importantly, the program level of lean thinking allows for inter-company process improvement, because the relationships are long-term ones, unlike the temporary nature of a single project. Furthermore, the level of innovation at the program level can be groundbreaking and yield significant enhancements in many areas such as resource planning and technology rollout. In this scenario, a dedicated team from the AE, a dedicated team from the GC, the trades, and the capital construction division of the power company can act as a single entity. The program is focused on improvement through a holistic perspective of cash conversion processes across company boundaries by combining the firm and the project elements. Lean thinking is applied to eliminate waste and improve operational consistency from project to project in many areas of the shaded zone in diagram below. Project managers for the contractor make decisions that result in improved overall performance for the business and related projects.

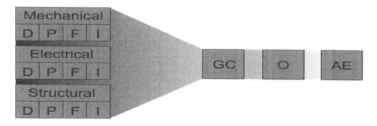

Notes: D = design activities, P = procurement activities, F = fabrication activities, I = installation activities, GC = general contractor, O = owner or plant manager, AE= architect/engineer.

5. Open lines of communication and collaboration. Lean thinking should be applied within an owner's construction program and should cross organizational boundaries through all design and build phases. The goal of lean thinking is to eliminate waste and improve operational consistency from project to project, as shown in the diagram above. Looking at the whole North American construction industry, the program level of lean thinking is less common, although there are some examples among underground utilities companies and their service providers. These examples provide the foundation necessary to form a holistic lean construction supply chain.

Beginning the Lean Journey

Some organizations have begun their lean journey at the firm level by transforming their operations and later adding field productivity and other lean aspects as they participate alongside other firms on a plant wide project. Another approach is for a firm to become involved with a project, such as a retrofit or quick turnaround effort, in which one of the trades or the GC has adopted LPS or other integrated planning systems. Later, that firm can work backward to transform its organization internally (upstream) into a lean culture.

Experts agree that there is no single right approach. Deciding where to start; the firm, the project, and/or the program level should be the first step. Wherever you start, examples from other corners of the construction industry show that a lean transformation can take two to three years. Lean construction requires hands-on executive involvement, a commitment to action, and perseverance to cause the changes to stick.

Chapter 23: Manufacturing Process Versus the Construction

In the long term, both construction and manufacturing strive to add value to their products via high returns on investment; however, each employs different means to achieve this objective. In manufacturing, the lifecycle of a product on the market is long enough to develop related research and training capabilities. In construction, a product's lifecycle is the relatively short project duration, and thus it is more difficult to justify research and training.

Lack of investment is damaging to the construction industry's capacity for innovation in process and technology and threatens its competitiveness in local and global markets. Further, decision making in manufacturing planning is concerned with capacity optimization to combat the trade-off between future growth and machine depreciation. Equipment in construction is commonly seen as a resource that can be purchased or rented/leased for the project based on the appropriate time-value analysis. Contractors seek to minimize ownership and operation costs while ensuring equipment availability.

The extent of operations in manufacturing is well defined from the beginning. The components to be produced or purchased will change only if there is a drastic change in costs. In construction, the supply chain is more flexible. Subcontractors or the main contractor can perform operations based on the resources and costs of each specific project. Similarly, the workforce in manufacturing generally enjoys more stable wage policies and higher employment security. Positions are well defined and people gain ample experience in performing specific tasks. In the construction industry, wages vary depending on skill, experience, and employers. Job security is low, and workers perform a range of tasks throughout the development of a project. The manufacturing industry has shown how experience and specialized skills are valuable, highly regarded, and well compensated.

Quality in manufacturing is related more closely to process control than to product conformance. Common tasks are defect prevention, monitoring, and intervention. Rework is generally avoided, and in some cases, parts are discarded rather than reprocessed. In contrast, quality in construction primarily related to product conformance. Specifications and drawings determine quality standards, and quality assurance is the joint effort of the construction company and the owner to meet safety requirements, environmental considerations, and conformance with applicable regulations. Rework is a common practice because only one final product will be delivered.

Supply in manufacturing is an order-driven activity that is synchronized through material handling systems. The operations sequence in manufacturing is determined during the product design phase, and changes are limited by the determined layout. Supply in construction is schedule driven because the process span is longer and the sequence of tasks can be modified, if required, by unforeseen exceptions. The construction supply chain is main-contractor-client based. Subcontracting can account for most of the value of the project and because project activities are totally interrelated, the relationship between subcontractors and the general contractor demands much cooperation and transparency.

Chapter 24: Barriers to Implementing Lean Construction in the United Kingdom

Lean construction management efforts could prove to be highly rewarding for the United Kingdom's (UK) construction industry. This was emphasised by the Egan Committee who stated that the concepts of Lean thinking would lead the UK construction industry's quest to improve quality and efficiency. Although various countries worldwide gained large benefits by adopting Lean Construction (LC) concepts, there still seems to be limited implementation of Lean in the UK construction industry, over the last two decades, even after the publication of the Egan report.

There appears to be a number of structural and cultural barriers that are militating against its successful implementation. By not realising the factors that affect the successful implementation of LC, organizations will not be able to know what improvement efforts need to be made, where these efforts should be focused, or which efforts could obtain best results. For this reason, this study sought to identify and assess the possible barriers to the successful implementation of LC in the UK. Based on an extensive literature review, followed by a statistical analysis of data gained from a questionnaire survey which targeted practitioners in the UK construction industry, a number of barriers were identified as key barriers. Further analysis revealed that only three of these barriers were determined as significant.

The results of this study could be used to help researchers, practitioners and companies in the UK construction industry to focus their attention and resources on the significant issues, crucial to support the successful implementation of LC.

Since 1998, efforts to encourage the use of Lean concepts in construction across most geographical areas of the UK has been growing, as exemplified in seminars staged by the Construction Industry Research and Information Association (CIRIA) and Construction Productivity Network (CPN). These efforts have been expanded to include the Construction Lean Improvement Programme (CLIP) that was created by the BRE in 2003 to promote case studies developed by Construction Excellence.

The establishment of the Lean Construction Institute UK (LCI-UK) and some Lean Construction (LC) consultancy and promotional companies has also helped to enhance awareness of LC principles. Some organizations and universities now offer LC education, which has been helpful in moving Lean thinking into the mainstream of construction education.

Despite these continuous efforts, a study by Common et al. (2000) has shown that the presence of a Lean culture within large UK construction companies is significantly less than that professed. An even larger gap is evident from the level of development recognized in the LC literature review in other countries, in comparison to those in UK (Common et al., 2000).

Although various countries gained large benefits by adopting LC concepts, there seems to be little implementation of Lean in the UK construction industry, over the last two decades, even after the publication of the Egan report. There appears to be some structural and cultural barriers that prevent its successful implementation.

The construction industry has rejected before many ideas from manufacturing because of the belief that construction is different; that is as projects in construction are one-off project based, more complex and take place under lots of uncertainties and constraints.

There is a repeated claim that the construction industry is very different than manufacturing because every product is unique. I do not agree with that claim because I believe that the construction industry includes lots of repeated processes. The task force suggests that the construction industry has two options; to ignore all this in the belief that construction is so unique that there are no lessons to be learned; or seek improvement through re-engineering construction, learning as much as possible from those who have done it elsewhere. These types of barriers are just temporary; they may slow down the diffusion but will not impede it.

Several studies have been carried out in different countries worldwide to identify the barriers in implementing the LC approach. Some of these studies focused on investigating barriers that prevent the diffusion and implementation of LC. Others focused on identifying barriers that exist during the execution of LC practices. These barriers could affect the application process of LC and hinder the project performance, if not properly managed. By not understanding the factors that affect the successful implementation of LC, organizations will not be able to know what improvement efforts need to be made, where these efforts should be focused, or which efforts could obtain best results.

Below are ten classified barriers to implementing Lean Construction.

1. Fragmentation and subcontracting

Many similar factors in the construction industry of both developed and developing nations act as an obstacle to the adoption of LC concepts. In both arenas, fragmentation and subcontracting in construction hinder the incentive for project participants to cooperate and learn together. These participants have different circumstances and priorities, but with one shared objective of successfully completing the related project; therefore, it is essential to establish effective communication between all parties by embarking on the partnering and integrated team-working route. That is because, in the process of implementing the LC concepts, poor communication will have a negative impact on the effectiveness of the project delivery and coordination system.

Additionally, in construction projects, contractors traditionally hire subcontractors. These subcontractors generally do not have contracts with the client; and may sometimes have to work with insufficient budgets, even if the client pays a fair price to the main contractor. As a result, this often leads to compromised quality of work. Although, some clients have tried to overcome these barriers by providing framework opportunities and partnering contracts, these usually only involve the main participants.

2. Procurement and contracts

Traditional Procurement methods and contracts undermine the application of Lean principles, because they seem to create adversarial relationships between parties involved and can add waste to the process. Contract forms that allow one party to impose power over another create adversarial relations. These adversarial relations create transaction costs which are considered waste, and are thus opposing to the Lean philosophy.

Any procurement form that tends to delegate design work to external designers, without any follow-up or incorporation, separates the design from the construction process; and therefore misses the Lean aim of collaboration and integration therefore, selecting a collaborative procurement system with a significant emphasis on concurrent design and construction, would be recommended for the successful implementation of LC.

3. Culture and human attitudinal issues

Applying Lean thinking principles into the construction industry requires a fresh approach in thinking about the complete process; in order to remove 'waste', create 'continuous flow', and radically enhance 'value' to the customer. On contrast, the culture of the UK construction industry is known to be opportunistic, prone to conflict and resistant to therefore, changing traditions and behaviour seems to be a necessary prerequisite for implementing LC in the UK. Factors such as lack of commitment, lack of ability to work in group, lack of self-criticism, weak communication and transparency among teams of the production process, cultural issues in getting the subcontractors and workers to adopt the methodology in a comprehensive way, fear of taking risk, wrong attitude to change, not viewing housekeeping as a continuous effort, lack of team spirit among professionals, over-enthusiastic champions, dependency, lack of incentives and motivation, lack of trust, and fear of blame and contractual disputes.

4. Adherence to traditional management concepts due to time and commercial pressure

One of the main barriers to the successful implementation of LC is the tendency of construction firms to apply traditional management concepts as opposed to productivity and quality initiatives. It seems that commercial pressure to do the deal takes place over production issues. For that reason, we advise companies not to wait for a crisis to make efforts to change; because it would be then too late to learn new skills and ways of thinking. We also stress that if construction firms keep stuck to their current management concepts, as they are satisfied with achieving their intended objectives, they will become reluctant to any changes even though these changes may help to improve their performance and increase their quality and productivity rates.

5. Financial issues

The successful implementation of LC requires adequate funding to provide relevant tools and equipment, sufficient professional wages, incentives and reward systems; investment in training and development programmes, and perhaps employing a Lean specialist to provide guidance to both employers and employees during the initial implementation. There are some common financial barriers that need to be carefully addressed. These include; inflation, inadequate funding of projects, unstable markets for construction, lack of basic sociable amenities required for facilitating the Lean implementation, lack of incentives and motivation, low professional remuneration, unwillingness of some companies to invest extra funds to provide training for their workers more than the essential legislation requirement.

6. **Lack of top management commitment and support**

The successful implementation of LC or any new innovative strategy needs to be supported by top management. Top managers have to provide sufficient time and resources to develop an effective plan, and manage changes arising from the implementation process. Lack of top management leadership and commitment is one of the main barrier to the implementation of LC, we believe that the problem exists with middle management not top management. For middle managers the benefits are not very clear and their training and experience is not sufficient to provide them with the ability to manage change in thinking, responsibility and roles. Alternatively, benefits for top management from implementing LC concepts are very clear; increased productivity, reduced time and accidents, however, several studies reported various management related issues such as; poor planning, lack of delegation to enhance work flow, poor understanding of customer needs, lack of a participative management style for the workforce, logistics' problems, absence of look-ahead planning and poor coordination.

7. **Design/ construction dichotomy**

Design and planning are identified as major attributes of the process of LC. Any ignorance to the importance of these could lead to disastrous loss of time, cost and the overall process. Due to traditional contractual procedures, design and implementation of design are treated as separate products. These causes a conflict border between the two phases and creates lots of waste such as; incomplete and inaccurate designs, rework in design and construction, lack of buildable designs, final products with significant variation from values specified in the design, and disruption to contractors due to design changes made by designers.

Designers usually ignore the production conditions in which their designs will be implemented. There is an argument on how to solve uncertainties of work on site and on how quality could be achieved. Some view the attainment of quality as a factor of relationships and good coordination, while others see it as a matter of strict adherence to specifications and codes.

A suggested solution to this design/construction dichotomy could be the use of the British Standard (BS) 5606:1990. The BS 5606 provides a formula for site personnel to calculate the consequences for the achievement of specified tolerances. Also, designers can make adjustments in their specifications to code recommendations if they anticipate circumstances on site that will make strict adherence to the code difficult or impossible; however, this still requires good collaboration and coordination between the two parties, and is subject to the multiple vagaries of inter-personal relations on. Another suggestion is giving the contractor the responsibility for the reinforcement detailing. Designers themselves acknowledged their limitation in producing buildable reinforced concrete designs; where poor detailing can account for about 20% of reinforcement which in turn is about 25% of the contract. This suggestion may lead to improved constructability, and gives the contractor some control during the design phase; this involvement could also encourage the takeup of Design and Build contracts.

One promising aspect is the tendency in the construction industry to adopt integrated design to enhance performance and add value to the final products. There are two opposing views regarding the way to adopt traditional design practices to the new trend of work (Forgues & Koskela, 2009). Promoters of sustainable construction hypothesize that it is a matter of developing from a sequential to an iterative design process; but the British government argues that a change to the context in which the design is realized is essential and requires a change in how projects are procured. The problem with integrated design team efficiency are related to context and not process, traditional procurement processes strengthen socio-cognitive barriers that hinder team efficiency, and new collaborative procurement approaches help to mitigate socio-cognitive barriers and improve integrated design team performance.

8. Lack of adequate Lean awareness/ understanding

Lean thinking principles have been adopted from manufacturing sectors to the construction industry therefore, many LC principles and techniques are referred to those contained within Lean manufacturing.

There is a debate on the extent to which methods of Lean production are applicable to LC. Some Lean production measures may not be equally applicable in construction and may need to be amended we suggest that it is essential to have a full comprehension about Lean manufacturing concepts in advance, in order to be able to clearly understand the concept of LC.

Additionally, many studies have reported the lack of exposure on the need to adopt LC, and difficulties in understanding its concepts to be significant barriers to the successful implementation of LC. This could be due to the lack of a shared and agreed definition or understanding of what is meant by Lean. Some experts does not agree with that claim because they believes that the definition and understanding of LC, as for other innovative management practices like partnering, would be best developed by investigating its core elements.

Furthermore, LC has introduced to the construction industry the usage of new tools which have a distinct difference when compared to those used in traditional practices. These differences have to be clearly understood in order for these tools to be optimally utilised; however, several researchers believe that Lean is more than tools or techniques; instead it requires a transformation in thinking, collaboration, flexibility, commitment, discipline, and a broad system-wide focus. Lean has to be implemented across the business and value chain to deliver the promised results; any isolated efforts may even cause waste.

A study by Common et al. (2000) revealed that there is a considerable lack of understanding to the fundamental concepts and application of Lean within UK construction companies. For instance, a majority of the respondents considered that the Lean concept is not suitable for the construction industry because of the demands from clients for quicker and cheaper projects. This is inconsistent with the principles of Lean of eliminating waste to reduce time and cost, and add value to the client. Also, many companies that professed to be applying LC principles seemed to combine traditional techniques with those that are considered Lean. A typical combination was the use of traditional contracting, critical path planning and supply chain management (SCM). Although SCM and partnering are important attributes to the successful implementation of LC, the use of traditional contracting and critical path planning (CPP) hinders their effects. That is because both traditional contracting and critical path planning have been identified as contributors of waste in construction. Furthermore, only a few companies recognized the importance of design and planning to the process of LC.

9. Educational issues

Although there have been several efforts to provide awareness and guidance to LC by researchers, academics, practitioners and professional bodies in the UK and some other countries, it seems that educational barriers could pose a great threat to the sustainable implementation of LC. Some of these barriers include; lack of technical skills, ignorance to human resource management and development, inadequate training, poor understanding and awareness, poor team-work skills, illiteracy and computer.

10. Lack of customer-focused and process-based performance measurement systems

There is an industry tendency to measure performance in terms of time, cost and meeting code; but very limited consideration has been subjected to client satisfaction. These traditional performance preferences measured in projects, specifically costs and schedule, are not appropriate for continuous improvement because they are not effective in identifying the root-causes of quality and productivity losses.

Traditional Performance measurement systems (PMSs) are based on financial measures. The latter are result-oriented performance indicators, and have been strongly criticised by many researchers. That is because these parameters are backward focused. They are not measured until project is complete; and thus the information obtained arrives too late to take any corrective actions. As a result, these outcome based indicators cannot be used to identify barriers or problems that exist during the execution of processes. Traditional control systems focus their attention in conversion activities and ignore flow activities; therefore nearly all non-value-adding activities become invisible.

We recommend the use of leading measures aiming to give early warnings, identify barriers and potential problems, and emphasize the need for future investigation. This recommendation is supported experts who asserted the need to adopt formal process based approaches. It is important to use measures for tracking improvement by detecting the problems and their root causes, not just reporting.

Lean construction (LC) efforts could prove to be highly rewarding for the UK construction industry. Although various countries worldwide gained large benefits by adopting the Lean concepts, it does not seem to be generally applied in the UK construction industry. There appears to be a number of structural and cultural barriers that are hindering the progress of UK construction organisations towards achieving the Lean approach.

Chapter 25: Lean Construction if Not Now, When?

Needless to say, the construction industry is badly broken and needs fixing. How does the industry rise up and meet the challenges of customer demand for higher quality, improved profitability, and the shortage of skilled workers? The first step is to cast aside the not invented here syndrome and embrace a time tested manufacturing solution; the Toyota Production System-commonly called Lean.

Why should construction company managers even consider Lean as a way to improve their business? Here are some eye opening facts about the U.S. construction industry:
1. 60% to 85% of construction time is spent waiting or fixing mistakes.
2. The average construction worker operates at 40% efficiency.
3. Critical shortages exist in qualified and skilled workers.
4. The return on equity for construction pales in comparison to all other U.S. industries.
5. Customers are frustrated with poor quality, confrontation, excessive change orders, and scheduling delays.

These are some of the same or similar issues Japanese companies like Toyota faced in the 1950's. Lean construction can help remediate the dire conditions described above. While Lean is no silver bullet, Lean construction offers substantial improvements to the problems facing the construction industry. If construction companies want to prosper in the 21st Century then they should move toward Lean thinking.

Why so Much Waste?

Why so much waste? Construction projects are so fragmented. Many times subcontractors do their work disregarding how what they do impact the work of other subcontractors. We call this the "throw it over the wall' mentality. One functional department (in this case subcontractor) completes its part of the project and throws it over the wall to the next department (subcontractor) who throws it back over the wall because it isn't right. This mentality sub-optimizes the performance of the entire project creating quality and schedule problems.

Lean thinking is a new way to manage construction. Many people object because they believe Lean is a manufacturing strategy and has no application in a "unique" industry like construction. The goal of Lean Process Improvement is to maximize value and eliminate waste using techniques like one-piece flow, Just-in-time delivery, and inventory reduction.

There is a small but growing movement to apply Lean principles to construction. Applying Lean principles to construction really means applying them to project management. This transformation involves mapping your construction processes, determining the most efficient work flow and establishing a pull system. How do you create a pull system? As a contractor you can begin by looking at what the completed project should be, and then work backwards, identifying each preceding step. Downstream processes determine what the upstream processes will be and when they should take place. Taking this view of the project will help you control the work flow. You should also look at creating value stream or process maps of your job support processes as well as project processes. Processes like job setup, estimating, payroll, accounts payable, purchasing, tool and material handling are good candidates for mapping.

The Need for Change

The construction industry is broken and the five facts below demonstrate why the industry needs to change:
1. If it takes six months to build a house, then 85 percent of the time is spent on two activities: waiting on the next trade to show up, and fixing mistakes.
2. Clemson's Professor Roger Liska conducted an analysis of productivity on the construction industry and found that the average construction worker operates at only 40 percent efficiency.
3. Critical shortages of qualified, skilled workers are predicted to only get worse.
4. Despite the construction boom of 2006, Business Week's 2007 Investment Outlook Report indicated the return on equity (ROE) for all U.S. industries was 17.9 percent, while the ROE for the construction industry was a mere 9.7 percent.
5. Industry customers are frustrated with poor quality, confrontation, excessive change orders in quantity and dollar value, scheduling delays and litigation.

Adding Value

Lean construction focuses on identifying and delivering products or services on which the client/owner places high value. Clients often place high value on:
1. No or limited change orders.

2. High quality meaning conformance to requirements and specifications.
3. On-time delivery of the project.

To learn what a particular client values, the contractor must effectively communicate, then collaborate, with the client to achieve those desired results. While it may be easier to accept this concept in the negotiated arena, it also works in the highly competitive bid marketplace.

While there are fewer options in the bid market than in the negotiated environment, there are still numerous ways contractors can add value to the construction process for owners that cost the contractor little or nothing. Simply by eliminating confrontation and reaching out through better communication and collaboration, the contractor can substantially increase value for the owner.

Profitability

When contractors focus on delivering maximum value to clients, they usually find that profit margins increase. This is not surprising, since in virtually any industry the cheapest products usually produce the smallest profit margin. Therefore, if a contractor competes on price, the contractor is forced into a low margin sector of the industry. Industry data supports the belief that highly competitive bid markets are the least profitable.

Secondly, since Lean construction is about reducing waste, this means lower costs. Therefore, the contractor is under less pressure to lower its profit margins. Toyota was able to almost immediately double its productivity. When you consider the average construction worker is working at only

40 percent efficiency, the construction industry should expect dramatic improvements. Before blaming the worker, it should be noted that the majority of the lost efficiency was due to poor management 20 percent results from waiting for materials or supplies, 20 percent results from inefficient company processes and 15 percent results from work rules or congested work areas.

Shortage of Skilled Workers

Another challenge the industry faces is a shortage of skilled workers. If the industry wants to attract workers, it must change the perception that construction work is undesirable. Again, Lean construction is a valuable tool in that battle. When there is a lack of workers, there is a tendency to reduce the job requirements to find additional workers. To make this work, the requirements tend to be revised downward so lower skilled workers can qualify. While this works in the short term, it creates boring jobs that highly skilled workers don't want. Further, this approach tends to reduce productivity and increase the downward pressure on wages because wages reflect productivity. Throwing money at a problem is never a solution, but wages are a factor in the equation. Therefore, emphasis must be placed on increased productivity so highly skilled workers can be attracted and wages increased. This isn't a delusion because Lean manufacturers have already proved this concept works.

While there are no panaceas, Lean offers substantial improvements to the challenges facing the construction industry. Those contractors that want to prosper in the 21st century should move toward thinking Lean to improve their processes.

The Power of Lean in Construction

Lean construction is a systematic application of Lean thinking to the design and construction of buildings that do what clients and end-users want-provide value. Evolved over the last 50 years, Lean thinking has revolutionized some parts of manufacturing and is now facilitating significant improvements in the way service organizations like hospitals, banks, etc. are meeting customer requirements.

Adopting Lean thinking requires sustained work over a number of years. There are no instant solutions. For most people, Lean requires a change in the way they think and the behaviours that support their actions. There are many things that Lean organizations do that can be copied; partnering, supply chain management, value stream analysis, flow, etc. but they are only Lean when they are done with Lean intent. That requires Lean thinking around how the organization works.

Not all construction firms accept waste as a necessary prerequisite for doing business. They minimize or eliminate it by using Lean tools and techniques. Lean process improvement isn't a new concept, but it is relatively new to construction. There are many sceptics who believe Lean is a manufacturing strategy and is not suited for the construction industry. Many aspects of the Toyota Production System and other Lean tools can and do apply to the construction process. Lean process improvement can reduce waste in construction with results mirroring other industries. Lean principles hold the promise of reducing or eliminating wasteful activities, costs, and inefficiencies in construction, creating a system that provides value to customers.

Chapter 26: Lean Construction Frequently Ask Questions

1. When did Lean Construction (LC) begin?

When current practice died; it died a slow death as the ideas and insights that form LC today came together. LC began with an insight that revealed the inability of the current planning system to produce predictable workflow. This was in the middle 1980s. A more formal start could be identified as the first meeting of the International Group for Lean Construction in 1993. We have no idea when LC will be completely defined let alone understood.

2. Is Lean Construction just applying Lean Production in construction?

No. The word "just" makes it sound as if Lean production itself were something small. Lean Construction started as an attempt to reform the way work in projects is managed. Once the obvious was understood, that work moves between specialist in construction by the administrative act of making an assignment, it was possible to adapt principles and practices direct from Toyota.

3. What is Lean Construction?

Lean Construction a different way to see, understand and act in the world. For example, waste in current practice is normally understood as labour utilization. Learning to see contingency as waste is the big step we need if we are to make a step change in construction, one commensurate with managing inventory just in time. Lean Construction is a philosophy; a comprehensive system of ideas that lead to the flawless delivery of the built environment. This philosophy is practiced using the Lean Project Delivery System, which continues to evolve as more is learned from practice and research. Lean Construction is the soil that allows us to "socially construct" the built environment. Lean Construction is something that people do; a philosophy or an orientation of sorts.

4. What are the major difference between a project run based on Lean Construction and one that is not?

Lean works because the work on the project is designed and managed by those who do it. LC designs and activates the network of commitments necessary to deliver the project. The "tragedy of the commons" is prevented; The individually rational decision is destructive to the overall project. The local optimization driven by labour utilization versus system optimization that is driven by throughput. Work on Lean Construction projects is deliberately and systematically organized to maximize the project and not the pieces, and commercial terms are adjusted to align interests, and promote improvement and minimize risk to the involved parties.

Another difference is that the construction process, the building operation and maintenance, and the recycling/salvage needs are inputs to the design and not outputs of it; inputs needed to start the work are provided and issues (waste) that prevent finishing started work are eliminated; problem solving and learning is the job of those involved in the project and not just part of the job; Where possible, materials are brought to the site in the same way concrete is; The aim is for a zero punchlist and not to zero-out the punchlist.

5. BIM aims to build a collaborative relation between designers and constructors, so how is that different from LC? BIM is technology. It doesn't aim, it does make possible different conversations. LC structures those conversations and connecting design, logistics and installation. LC designs and activates the network of commitments necessary to deliver the project. It is necessary to enable Lean Construction ideals but not sufficient.

6. Is Lean Construction like LEED where you have to commit to a certain level of compliance and the project is checked against that?

No. Lean is a way to manage and improve work. LEED and GREEN are value propositions; an end. Lean Construction is the means to better arrive at that end.

7. What percentage of the US construction industry is adopting it?

There is no way of knowing. Lots of hospitals, lots of suppliers etc. There is still time to be an early adopter.

8. Is Lean Construction accepted more in other countries than in the US?

We have no way of making a well grounded assessment. There is significant implementation in Germany, Denmark (the longest running with strong Union support, Sweden, Brasil, Chile and Peru. I would not say the US is ahead.

9. What is the primary difference between Lean Production and Lean Construction?

   a. Lean production is the inspiration for lean construction, but cannot be grafted onto construction.
   b. Production and construction are different; construction is more like ship building or airplane building, where the workers move and the product is stationary instead of the product moving between stationary workers like in production.
   c. In production, typically the same part is produced in mass volume. This is not the same as construction unless major generalizations are made (i.e. a wall is a wall, even if made of different material and on different projects). So, lean construction focuses heavily on the similarity in the process of constructing more so than on the product of construction.
   d. We need to move from construction on to project production in general because it sees the project as the basic form of production where mass production is just the simplified version Toyota and Shingo showed us new thoughts but we have to establish our own thinking.
   e. Lean Production primarily focuses on the reduction of the time from order, of any transaction be it assembly, billing, supply, etc, to delivery. This reduction of time is achieved by the elimination of waste (the unproductive use of resources) that is captured in "DOWNTIME". Respect for people and continuous improvement guides the reduction of waste. Lean Construction has been inspired by this but also by other paradigms. Production in construction is conceptualized as a transformation of

inputs to outputs through a flow process of materials and information that is directed at maximizing value to the client. Lean Production is not about maximizing value to the client, otherwise, we would have had the Cadillac for the price of the Chevy, the Lexus for the price of the Camry, etc.

Lean Construction also draws on the new theories regarding project management as well as social science, and complexity theory. A construction project is really a project based production system.

10. Can the concept of Heijunk a be used in construction? Why?

    a. Heijunka = production levelling. Production levelling for a manufacturing plant relies on being able to "create" stable demand, so that the Takt time for the plant is constant. Toyota does this through its marketing and sales division. The TPS is so vulnerable otherwise. Of course, it is not always perfect but they strive for this stability, especially with tactics such as mixed model production.

    b. In construction, we are project based and we know what needs to be done for a project; the quantities are known, with a time and budget constraint. What we need is stability and reliability in the workflow so that we are not going in fits and stops. We achieve this using the Look ahead and weekly work planning process with a constraint screening process, and not just an FYI coordination meeting. The act of keeping a workable backlog is designed to keep work flowing and progressing.

 c. The use of the line of balance (linear scheduling, flow lines) is a nice tool to visualize the production rates of different activity and avoid the interruption of work as well as the problem of overproduction. However, in Lean Construction we don't want to see one crew finish too fast or too slow.
 d. Crew balancing is not an example of heijunka. Crew balancing may lead us to locally optimize at the expense of the system throughput.

11. Contrast "lean work structuring" with "work breakdown structure".

 a. A WBS should not be used as the sole planning tool for a project. It is a great brainstorming tool to understand the project. It is probably the best scheme to develop a MASTER schedule. The problem is that we use it for more than what it is capable of. We can't determine project cost and project duration by simply working the WBS. The WBS is looking at activities in an independent fashion in support of transformation thinking. The WBS assumes that optimizing the part will optimize the whole; reduce the part cost and duration and you will reduce the cost and the duration of the whole. Get the lowest price and the shortest time for drywall separate from electrical and plumbing and you find on site that the work of these three trades is so intertwined that the cost and duration you received for drywall was a pipe dream.
 b. A WBS is a tool to use in Lean Work Structuring.
 c. LWS is thinking production, operation, maintenance, and recyclablity during design. It also focuses on work package (not trade or contract packages), i.e. the wall, or the ceiling.

12. What are the differences between project control and production control?

   a. Project control monitors progress using lagging indicators such as schedule and cost variance. It is sometimes too late to do anything about the project going off-track or it takes too much to get it back on track. So, project control is reactive. Think of the stock market. The DJI - Dow Jones Industrial Average - only tells you what has happened to the market after the fact. It's like taking the temperature of a patient; it tells you whether the person has a fever but not why.
   b. We need to practice production control such that we make things happen to prevent the project from having a fever. Production control is proactive in the sense that you are doing all that you can to make work happen by removing the constraints that you know about.

13. Is Value Stream Mapping (VSM) a tool for construction?

VSM has a place in construction. In fact, it is probably being implemented but we just don't know about it and this applies to many other tools and techniques that are being used to enable the lean construction ideals, but we don't know about them. The Last Planner System is one example.

As far as VSM is concerned, it provides a big picture view of the flow problems in whatever system you are studying. It's a flow improvement tool and not a process improvement tool (flow kaizen vs. process kaizen). A great bottleneck finder. VSM has been applied to reduce the time for processing specialty contractor payment applications (from 40 days to 5 or). An architecture office also is using it for streamlining the submittal and show drawings review and approval process because of delays and complaints by contractors. An example for application on a construction site is that of a construction company that specializes in suspended ceiling and drywall installation. They used VSM to identify time that drywall sheets and tiles spend before being put in place. They used the results to justify the cost of using a temp warehouse (supermarket) close to the site and deploying a pull delivery system (the best they could do). The result, using the SAME installation process, was less time per square feet because material handling was almost down to single Touch – from the truck to the installation location. Interestingly, they then used work sampling techniques to improve the drywalling process itself.

In Brazil, VSM is being used mostly by academics. As any other tool developed for manufacturing it needs some adaptation in order to become useful for construction.

14. Is Integrated Project Delivery the same as Lean Construction?

No. In fact, the ideals of Lean Construction are enabled by using the Integrated Project Delivery approach. IPD is necessary but not sufficient. In other words, just having an IPD will not guarantee that we meet the Lean Construction ideals.

IPD is a Relational Contracting approach that aligns project objectives with the interests of key participants, through a team based approach. The primary Team Members would include the Architect, key technical consultants as well as a general contractor and key subcontractors. It creates an organization able to apply the principles and practices of the Lean Project Delivery System.

Keep improving!!

Made in the USA
Lexington, KY
14 January 2015